Losing It

The Virginity Myth

Edited by
Louis M. Crosier

1993
AVOCUS PUBLISHING, INC.
WASHINGTON, D.C.

LOSING IT:
THE VIRGINITY MYTH
Edited by Louis M. Crosier

Published by:

Avocus Publishing, Inc.
1223 Potomac Street, NW
Washington, DC 20007 U.S.A.
(202) 333-8190
FAX: (202) 337-3809
Orders: (800) 345-6665

All rights reserved. No part of this book may be reproduced or transmitted in any form or by any means, electronic or mechanical, including photocopying, recording or by any information storage and retrieval system without the permission of the editor, except for the inclusion of brief quotations.

Disclaimer:

This book has no definitive answers. It provides a framework wherein the reader is invited to participate in expanding and defining his horizons. It contains experiences and opinion. Nothing contained in this book is intended in any way to be libelous in nature. Neither is it the intent of Avocus Publishing, Inc. to publish any accusatory statement, direct or implied, of improper motives or illegal actions by any individual, group or institution. We do not believe and have not intended to assert that anything contained herein represents a sinister movement, or that persons associated therewith are a disgrace to themselves or to society. Any other interpretation of our printing is erroneous and therefore misunderstood. All names of individuals have been changed or omitted except in the professional commentaries.

Copyright © 1993 by Avocus Publishing, Inc.
Printed in the United States of America

Library of Congress Catalog Card Number: 93-71214

ISBN 0-9627671-3-1 (Hardcover) $19.95
0-9627671-2-3 (Softcover) $12.95

For Sam and Tess

With Love

Contents

	Preface *by Louis M. Crosier*	1
	Foreword: **Healthy Choices** *by Trish Moylan Torruella, Director of Education, Planned Parenthood Federation of America*	3
1	**"Love Boat" Surprise** *by Emmy Farnsworth*	7
2	**Pop** *by Roger Healy*	13
3	**The Wrath of God** *by Madeleine Cummings*	19
4	**Batman, Hot Dogs and the Ultimate Zucchini** *by Chris Fischer*	25
5	**Boys Will Be Boys** *by Braxton Brittle*	31
6	**Performance: What's Likely to Happen** *by Dennis M. Dailey, D.S.W., Professor, University of Kansas School of Social Welfare*	41
7	**Love in Black and White** *by Nancy Brown*	45
8	**The Myth** *by Shelley Lapree*	53
9	**Yearning for That Big Moment** *by John Mason*	63
10	**STDs and AIDS** *by Peggy Clarke, Executive Director, American Social Health Association*	67
11	**In Search of a Definition** *by Jack Watson*	71
12	**Don't Blow It** *by Richard James*	77
13	**The Same Little Girl from New England** *by Anna Magdelena*	97
14	**What My Parents Didn't Tell Me** *by Sybil Joy*	103
15	**Outercourse: A Pleasure-Oriented Model of Sexual Expression** *by Beverly Whipple, PhD., RN, FAAN*	109
16	**Pump!** *by Charlie Cripton*	113
17	**The Game** *by Connie Maple*	119
18	**Reasons to Wait** *by Patrick F. Bassett, President, Independent School Association of the Central States*	125

19	**Sweet 16** *by Roxanne Connors*	129
20	**AIDS and Early Sexual Experience** *by J.D. Robinson, M.D.*	135
21	**Choice** *by Tilly Goldman*	139
22	**Virgin** *by Sarah Hardin*	143
23	**Date Rape** *by Patricia Sole*	149
24	**Communicating Sexuality** *by Caryl T. Moy, MSW, Ph.D.*	157
25	**Patience is a Virtue** *by M. Hunter Marks*	161
26	**Despite a Harvard Education** *by Jacqueline Walsh*	167
27	**Condoms, Failure Rates, and the "M" Word** *by Mary H. Devaney, Director, Parents for Prevention*	177
28	**Hurricane Helen** *by Stuart Ellis*	181
29	**With a Little Help from My Friends** *by Bea Graham*	187
	Conclusion: Is Virginity Important? *by Dr. Barry McCarthy, American University and Washington Psychological Center*	191

Preface

Losing It will encourage people to closely examine their own sexuality, the origin and evolution of their sexual values and the impact of those values on their attitudes and behavior. Presently, the goal-oriented approach to sex so often associated with a male mentality obscures healthy sexual interaction and leaves people feeling victimized or dissatisfied. This book will succeed if it helps people approach sexuality in a healthier, more responsible and pleasurable way.

Losing It suggests that relationships are most likely to be fulfilling when based on a foundation of communication between partners and an understanding of personal needs. This approach permits transcendence of gender stereotypes, peer pressure and fears which can prevent relationships from becoming mutually satisfying. Ultimately, I hope the book will redefine virginity, open up classroom and family discussions and encourage partners to talk about the risks and opportunities associated with sex.

In particular, more open discussion about sexuality will heighten awareness of AIDS, unwanted pregnancy and sexual abuse. More and more of America's high school and college students from every background are infecting each other with HIV, the virus which has proven to be non-discriminatory and far more prevalent than attitudes toward sexual behavior would suggest. Teen pregnancy continues at an alarming rate. Date rape and other forms of sexual abuse are only beginning to get the attention they deserve. When people become more comfortable talking about sexuality, more informed reflection will hopefully replace impulsive behavior and lead to more responsible and emotionally satisfying experiences.

Avocus Publishing produces group-authored books on timely social issues. The goal is to encourage meaningful dialogue and promote healthy, responsible behavior. I hope this book helps you examine your own values and initiates a conversation you can continue with friends and family.

Louis M. Crosier

Foreword

Healthy Choices

by Trish Moylan Torruella
Director of Education
Planned Parenthood Federation of America

With startling poignancy, this collection of personal accounts about losing one's virginity clearly illustrates that the process of sexual initiation and learning is natural, universal—and seldom easy. Each of these voices—male and female, gay and straight—reminds us that our first coital experience has profound developmental significance. What is equally evident in this collection, but less readily acknowledged in our society because it is unsettling, is that our rites of passage are often confusing and lonely experiences.

In a society reluctant to recognize adolescent sexuality, and driven by fear of the risks associated with sexual activity, young people are left to themselves to make sense of multiple and contradictory messages about sexuality. Their changing bodies and feelings send powerful, nonverbal messages about the potential that sex holds for pleasure and connection. In the best of all possible worlds, these internal sources of information are balanced by external ones—families, schools, religious institutions, and health professionals—who, in sensitive, caring, and responsible ways provide consistent guidance on the developmental journey.

Unfortunately, the real world is populated by adults who themselves have not had the benefit of such support in learning—or teaching—about sexuality in proactive, positive ways. Parents, anxious to protect their children, but uncomfortable in their role as sexuality educators, communicate their ambivalence through embarrassed silence or through cryptic prohibitions about sexual activity ("just say 'No'"); schools, mired in controversy and compromise about the content of courses offered in grades K–12, leave young people without access to comprehensive, accurate information and opportunities for skill-development; religious and other institutions are influential but seldom objective sources of attitudes and values about sexual issues; and health professionals, trained to prevent and to treat illness, approach sexuality from a largely clinical perspective.

Filling the vacuum left by families and social structures, the media has become the dominant available teacher. Music, videos, movies, and television are pervasive, entertaining, and compelling sources of information for young people that shape—and distort—the adolescent's view of the world and of relationships. Unfortunately, media images and messages are more often based in fantasy than in reality, likely to promote gender stereotypes, and ill-equipped to help young people negotiate the challenges and complexities of life in the 90s.

In the absence of other reliable sources, it is natural and common for adolescents to turn to friends for information and validation. While peers are important companions, they, too, are subject to the incomplete, ambiguous, and contradictory messages about sexuality that abound. And they can hardly be depended upon as reliable sources for information and guidance.

What *do* young people need in order to make healthy choices? They need:

Life Options

Adolescents who are hopeful about their lives and clear about their goals and options are far more likely to value themselves and to make decisions that serve their best interests. Motivation to make healthy choices is inextricably linked to a young person's self-perception and self-esteem. Adolescents need the vision of a successful future combined with information and skills in order effectively to prevent the negative consequences of sexual activity and lead sexually healthy lives.

Communication Skills

Adolescents need safe spaces and trusted, knowledgeable adults with whom to have an ongoing discussion—not a one-time "talk"—about the role that sexuality plays in their lives and in growing up. In the context of these mentoring relationships, young people learn to ask questions, clarify confusion, describe feelings and express needs without fear of judgment or ridicule, and make decisions. In the process of finding out who they are, young people need to know that they are not alone, that differences are normal, and that being sexually healthy is a lifelong endeavor.

Access to Information and Health Services

Accurate, balanced information about the full range of sexual issues—including sexual identity and orientation, sexual response, relationships, communication, intimacy, pleasure, sexual and reproductive health, and safer sex—is an essential component in making healthy decisions. And in order to be useful, information and services must be appropriately geared to the developmental levels of different adolescents, as well as to the diversity of their cultural backgrounds, family structures, sexual orientations, and lifestyles. Ensuring this access is an important job best shared by significant adults—parents, teachers, clergy, youth leaders, and health professionals—who have made a conscious effort to equip themselves for the responsibility.

Awareness of Rights and Responsibilities

Choosing whether or not to have sex is a right that cannot be imposed or taken away by another person. A sexual decision is not healthy if it is dishonest, exploitive or coerced. Nor is it healthy if it puts an adolescent at risk for an unintended pregnancy or sexually transmitted infection. Since all sexual decisions have consequences, the right to sexual expression carries responsibility—the responsibility to be informed, to communicate, and to be prepared to live with the outcomes of our sexual choices.

1

"Love Boat" Surprise

by Emmy Farnsworth

I lost my virginity 10 years ago next month. I'm 26 now. During the past ten years I've had sex with 11 different people: 1 failed fiancee, 4 steady boyfriends, 2 close "platonic" friends, 1 casual boyfriend, 1 guy I was trying to turn into a boyfriend but didn't, 1 slight acquaintance while under the influence of an obscene amount of alcohol, 1 date rape, and a partridge in a pear tree. (Dumb joke, sorry, it's just that even starting to think back about all this has made me very nervous.)

I only recount these statistics because statistics have been important to me in dealing with my sex life. I have always scoured the popular press for results of polls and surveys about sexual practices, searching for clues about how I should be. "Cosmopolitan" Magazine alone is a treasure trove of useful facts, "How many dates are you supposed to have with someone before you sleep with them? How many partners does the average American woman have before she marries? How many women have been sexually assaulted? What's normal out there?" On the many occasions when I've felt dirty and regretful about my sexual history, I've relied on these numbers for reassurance. They tell me that everyone makes mistakes, maybe not as many as I have, but mistakes nonetheless.

I had been dating my high school boyfriend Jim for about three months when he started to ask about sex. We had kissed a lot and had a few furtive fondlings above the waist, you know, kid stuff. But sex? No, sex was something that had never occurred to me. Sex was something that uptight, over-achieving, suburban sixteen year old girls just did not do, right? I told him it was out of the question.

Amazingly enough, he seemed fine with my decision. He was kind and calm about it, saying words to the effect of, "We'll wait till you're ready." He'd mention it again every once in a while, but I honestly didn't feel like he was giving me the hard sell. Jim was a cool guy.

I wasn't the only one who liked Jim. His family was new in town which made him exotic. He was cute, athletic, smart, POPULAR and captain of the track team and somehow, inexplicably, he fell for geeky old me.

Before Jim, my Saturday evening companions had been the folks on Fantasy Island and The Love Boat ("Oh Julie, I know I've only known you for two days, but we have had some spectacular sex and you seem real nice so why don't we elope right this very minute and live happily ever after, OK?"). I sat there eating cheese curls and vaguely yearning that Gopher would jump off the screen and whisk me away from my lonely toil with pre-calculus and French III.

Now that I had this great guy who liked me, I (we) was invited to movie-outings, parties, and concerts. I got to stand in the cheering-girlfriend section at the track meets and when he won everyone hugged me too. He gave me these great gold earrings for Christmas, and my friends were all so jealous. Somewhere during all this a light bulb must have gone off in my head telling me that having a popular boyfriend made me popular too. Slowly this message twisted and turned into an unconscious mandate—you will only be liked if you have a boyfriend, you must have a boyfriend. Do not let this person go. Needless to say, self-esteem has never been my strong suit.

At the beginning of February, Jim started making jokes about wouldn't it be something to remember if we lost our virginity on Valentine's Day.

"Ha, ha," I giggled back, "You know how I feel about the whole thing."

He must have grumbled his kindly grumble a bit more aggressively this time. Whatever the clue was, I inferred that he was getting impatient with my reluctance, maybe even impatient enough to look for action elsewhere. That same week, I came across my first statistical sex survey. It said that the average age for American girls to have sex was 16.4 years old. I was already a couple of weeks past that, so maybe it would be OK. Maybe having sex now was the "normal" thing to do.

On Valentine's Day, I wrote him a touching teenage love sonnet and told him I'd sleep with him. I had no clue what I was getting myself into, or more accurately, I had no clue what would be getting into me. I had never seen a naked man before. I had never touched a penis. I had never been touched below the waist. I didn't even masturbate. Sex was just not part of my thinking. Neither the mechanics nor the emotional consequences had ever occurred to me. I intended to treat sex as you would a mountain lake—there's no reason to stick your toe in and test the waters, you already know it's going to be a shock.

Two days later Jim told me after school that his Mom would be gone until after supper and why didn't we have sex then. Not seeing any way out of it, I said yes.

We undressed quickly in the half dark. He tried to be nice and get me to relax, but I just couldn't. I spent the next little while visibly shivering. At the time I convinced myself I was cold. In retrospect I can see I was terrified. So, I was scared, and he was a raging bull of teen testosterone, and then it was over—I don't remember the details very clearly.

What I do remember was lying in bed at home that night thinking that I should feel somehow different or special or magical or something. But I didn't. I just felt like me. The next day in school, I walked around looking at people trying to see if I could spot other ex-virgins. Later that week, my father, with great clarity of hindsight, came out of the blue with a proclamation that sex was not an option, ever, while I lived in his house. No provocation, no discussion.

Maybe I had gotten it into my head that if I did it once I'd never have to do it again, but Jim sure didn't have that idea. When I had sex with Jim, I created a monster. Each day was a new adventure, new lies to my parents about where I had been, new levels of fear about getting caught in not-so-private places, new degrees of physical pain (it didn't seem to matter if I was "ready" for sex). All this was normal, at least that's what they said in "Cosmopolitan." Right?

We always used condoms, but on two separate occasions my period was several weeks late. I made Jim go to a CVS in the next town to buy the home pregnancy test. I thought my head would explode waiting for the results. I wanted to crawl into a hole and die; Jim wanted to have sex, so we did. I didn't end up being pregnant, thank God. I'm sure my body was just too stressed out and confused to menstruate.

At the end of the year, Jim took me to his prom, the SENIOR prom. I was one of only three junior girls who was invited. What a coup this was.

Jim went away to college; everyone knew he would. There were many weekends he'd hitchhike home to see me. I had a boyfriend in college. I must be special.

The next spring I was accepted at the very same college. My parents hadn't thought I'd get in and were worried I was in over my head. My friends congratulated me for having found a way to be with Jim. As I flip through my high school yearbook right now the messages inscribed by my friends say, "I hope that things will go well for you and Jim at school," "That's how you're remembered at my house, the girl who came here to dinner with the guy who's in college," "I know you'll always be with Jim, you guys are such the perfect couple." It's a wonder I even knew my own name.

Not long after I got to college, Jim broke up with me. He had outgrown his hometown honey. I was despondent. How could I be without a boyfriend? Who would be my friend? Who would I be?

I quickly attached myself to a guy in my theater group, Gary. He was nice enough and seemed sympathetic to my situation—he was going through a breakup with his high school sweetheart who was also there at college with us. After a late rehearsal, he offered to walk me home, but somehow we ended up at his dorm. His roommates were nowhere to be found.

Again, the details of the encounter are fuzzy to me. My subconscious had done an excellent job of burying my deep dark secrets. I do remember him kissing me and then trying to reach under my skirt. I know I backed away and told him I was frightened. I know I said I wasn't ready to have sex with him. He said there was nothing to worry about, he would take care of me. Then he put his hand over my mouth and pushed me to the floor. I had never heard of date rape. He said it was all right, so this must be normal. Why was I back in my room crying half an hour later?

For the next three weeks, he'd screw me silently in the middle of the night, telling me it was our little secret. My "Love Boat" mentality still had me thinking that if you had sex with a boy, that meant he wanted to be with you, he wanted you to be the central character in his life. So I kept asking Gary when we would get to go out to dinner, when he would take me to the movies, when he would hold my hand? And for the next three weeks he told me we could not be seen on a "date" because it might hurt his old girlfriend's feelings to see us together. I tried to sit with him and his friends at the dining hall, but he took me aside and told me firmly I could not sit with them, I could not visit him during the day, and he would not say hello to me if he saw me on campus. His old girlfriend might be hurt.

The way he said everything, it made perfect sense. She was beautiful, his family loved her, they were meant to be together. I should just go away. So I did. Obviously, I was not as good as she.

In retrospect, I can see these first experiences with sex sent me into a vicious cycle. I saw that I had more friends and more attention when I had a boy, and I was told that I was not as worthy as other girls so I'd better put out in order to keep a boy.

With this always in the back of my mind, I went through a long string of boyfriends in college. The pattern was simple: I would flirt with some guy I knew slightly from a class or activity, we'd have sex very early in the relationship, and then I'd attach myself to him like a barnacle on a pier. I'd adopt all his interests, follow him all over campus, and concoct these little schemes to get him to tell me he loved me. We would always have lots of sex because that's what he wanted and that's what happy couples were supposed to do. "Cosmo" said so.

For a while, this would work. I'd get to hang out with his friends, and he'd think I was great until he realized I was boring and had no identity of my own, so we'd break up. This part took a while, sometimes years.

Actually, it was almost always me who did the ending of things. My ego was much too fragile to withstand getting dumped. Whenever I sensed that things were getting bad, I'd find another guy, sleep with him and get the cycle going again, and then break up with the first guy. That way, I never had to be alone. I was very proud to say that in over nine years, I had never been more than two weeks between boyfriends. I was a prized commodity; everyone wanted me.

The most recent of these relationships was Mark. He not only had an ex-girlfriend he was trying to protect, but also insisted we have sex in public places no matter what I said. He was perfect. For the longest time I thought I loved him. Maybe I did love him, it's hard for me to judge these things anymore.

A couple of years ago, I started to have panic attacks during the night. I'd wake up shivering when it was 80 degrees, hyperventilating and not breathing at the same time, terrified to be alone. Mark probably saved my life at that point by letting me know that these attacks were not normal (uh oh, we can't have that) and that maybe I should see a therapist.

I only saw this therapist for about six weeks. At the time I didn't think she could help me. She kept telling me I didn't have to stay with Mark if I didn't like what we were doing. She kept telling me no one would really respect me until I respected myself. She told me I had a problem with self-esteem. Why was I paying this woman to tell me these lies? Boys liked me, I must be an OK person.

I went back to my relationship with Mark and stopped telling him about the panic attacks. Then, six months ago, after about a dozen sleepless nights, it dawned on me that maybe the shrink was right. I don't think there was any one thing that made me realize this, it was probably years in the making.

I now live 1,500 miles away from Mark and everyone else I ever slept with. I've ditched my whole life—job, relationship, paid-for furniture—and started over. I'm in graduate school now. I'm doing well in my program and have made some good friends. People like me all by myself. I get asked to parties, movies and concerts even if I don't have a date. This is the happiest I've been in a very long time.

I realize I might have left the impression that I've been constantly victimized, led a miserable life, and hate sex. This is not the case, I've had some wonderful, caring sexual experiences. And now that I'm learning to appreciate my own accomplishments, I can be proud of many academic, social, and career achievements. Most of my unhappy sexual experiences have been because of my own bad judgment. I did what I thought I was supposed to and not what felt right for me.

People always talk about peer pressure. I never talked to my peers much about sex (I'm pretty sure that most of my high school classmates remained virgins well into college). I relied on the media to tell me what I should be doing. TV, movies, and magazines made it seem so simple. Everyone was having sex and all sex had a happy ending.

I see this ten year anniversary of losing my virginity as a milestone—a good time to take stock of where I've been and where I want to be going. I think I'm going to cancel my subscription to "Cosmopolitan."

2

Pop

by Roger Healy

I was looking for nirvana. Ever since I had my first morning stiffy and an idea of what sex was, I knew I wanted my first carnal escapade to be perfect. At 12 years old, the thought of losing my virginity was simply the balls, and I began rehearsing the event in my mind.

The revelation came rapidly. As recently as the previous year, I had been fixated on my birthdays. The anticipation of opening presents and eating cake meant several sleepless nights. The thought of an unbridled Christmas morning was rapture. At 12, my obsession turned to pussy. Birthday cake lost its luster, and my concentration shifted to my first bone. With the aid of an occasional glimpse in a magazine of a pair of bodacious tatas next to the pool at Mansion West, I built the glamorous idea that sex must be nothing less than pure bliss and that I was going to make my first experience the ultimate.

Licentious thoughts aside, I was also preoccupied with romance. I wanted my first experience to be accompanied by love. I decided I was going to find the right girl, wait for the perfect moment, create the perfect atmosphere, and have unbelievable sex. Losing my virginity by having a sexual experience at least equal to my wildest dreams was an ideal I held onto for years.

* * *

My early adolescence was active sexually—though I stuck to my plan of saving myself for the right moment while playing doctor with the 12 year old girls next door. Although they were isolated incidents, I actually had a few opportunities to have sex in my early teens, but held back partly because I wanted to wait for the "right girl at the right age," and partly because naked flesh was a little more ominous in person than in pictures. This didn't bother me because everything was on track. I was popular, confident and making girl friends.

But then disaster struck. Puberty hit me with a much worse case of zits than any of my friends, and as the zits came, the confidence drained. Pressure, partly from friends and partly self-inflicted, contributed to the problem as well. The number of bases that a teenage boy covered was a measure of his manhood and acceptance, and knowing this made an anxious boy even more nervous. High school was one long and ugly dry spell. Although I still had sex on the brain, I didn't have it anywhere else, and there was a stretch of four years where I didn't even kiss a girl. Looking back, I had a few opportunities to start a relationship but botched the job each time. I was out of practice and lacking confidence.

When college rolled around, my zits faded and my confidence returned. At least some of it. At the end of my freshman year I met Nancy. She was great, or at least great for me at the time. She was responsive enough to make me feel I could bust-a-move without rejection and aggressive enough to take the first step when I didn't. I wasn't a great boyfriend though, as I spent more time focusing on making up for the past four years than on building a personal relationship. I was still caught up in the male adolescent "pussy mentality," where sex topped the list of priorities in a relationship. The month of dating was fun, but it didn't end like a story book. We both came to the realization that the main thing we found interesting in the affair was each other's bodies. Not that there is anything evil about that, but we both wanted a relationship.

I set out to find "Miss Right," someone who had the same interests, who was fun, pretty and possible marriage material, someone who made me tingle. I kept my eyes open and looked hard, but the next two years turned out as dry as before. Few women I met appeared to fit the bill, and those who did ended up being taken, out of my reach, not "Miss Right" after all, and in one case, a lesbian. It was 1985, and I was 20. The vast majority of my friends had now lost their virginity and I was starting to get nervous. I wanted to find the right girl, but also wanted to be normal. I was anxious and didn't understand why meeting someone was so difficult. It didn't seem hard for my friends, and the AIDS threat was not yet a great concern to my heterosexual classmates, so I began to worry that I wasn't attractive. I was thin so started to lift weights. I needed to meet new people so started to go to more parties. However, when I approached women, I was nervous and had trouble starting things off. I had set myself up for rejection a few times, and rejection was what I got. I became much more cautious in approaching the dating topic, as I didn't want to get turned down any more with the same result as before—nothing. Things didn't look up until that summer.

Rachel. She was a fellow summer intern at the bank where I worked, and she was perfect. We quickly progressed from colleagues to friends, and spent our lunches together and played tennis (my big sport) after work. She was nice, gorgeous, enchanting, had similar interests and made me tingle. After a few weeks of building a friendship, I decided to risk my pride and bust-a-move. This time I would plan out everything to the minutest detail so nothing could screw up. I asked her to dinner and made reservations at several restaurants for the same night so I could choose the right one at the last moment. We went out and had a pretty good evening (I was very nervous but didn't screw anything up). When I dropped her home, she stood there giving me an opening, waiting for a kiss. But I froze. I told myself I would rather wait and make sure everything was perfect before I made my approach. We were standing on the street, and something just didn't seem right.

The next week was filled with phone calls and flowers left on her desk. I bought her favorite cake and had it sent to her apartment. In a week I had changed from easy-going friend to suitor in very hot pursuit. I took a photograph of us, had it enlarged and framed and put it on her desk at work with a personal note on the back. I think that was the last straw; I had gone overboard. And before I had that "next chance" I had been waiting for, I had scared her away. Looking back, I don't blame her. I did go nuts, but I just wanted everything to be right.

A few days later I was in the car with my dad going away for the weekend and was depressed. We have a close relationship, so I felt comfortable talking to him. I turned and said, "Pop, I'm depressed. I've been saving myself for the right girl. I've been waiting so long already. I still want to find the right one, but each time I think I've found someone, I screw it up. I'm worried I'll never find a girlfriend." Then I proceeded to tell him what had happened with Rachel.

"Let me tell you a story," was his response. "Imagine that you break your leg and can't play tennis. While you have your cast on, you dream about getting a chance to play a match. You watch the pros on TV and build the image in your mind that you might play that well when you get back on the court. Your cast finally comes off and you start to walk around, loosening up. Someone asks you to go out and hit, but you say "no." Your logic is that you've gotten yourself excited for a good match, so you don't want to go out there hobbling around the court, you'd rather wait 'til you can play a good game. Your leg gets better, but now it's winter so you decide you might as well wait for spring. Because you've waited so long for a great tennis match already, you don't want to accept second best and play indoors, so you spend the winter watching tennis on TV, convincing yourself that your strokes are similar to those in your imagination. Then spring comes, and it turns out to be too windy, too cloudy, too chilly, or you just don't have the right opposition, so you keep putting off your return to tennis. Then a perfect weekend day in the summer comes along. It's sunny and 78 degrees. You're asked to play in a weekend tournament with a great partner and an impressive list of opponents. You pull your racquets out of your bag, stretch out, and leap onto the courts, ready for action. You play the absolute worst tennis of your life.

"Why? Because you are completely out of practice. You haven't played in two years! And that's what's happening to you when you try to go on a date. You wait for the perfect girl, but when she comes along, you don't know what to do because you have never done it before. You tense up, lose your confidence, overplay the situation, and before you know it, you're waiting for the next ''perfect'' relationship to come along so you can ruin that too. Here's what you have to do. Go out, find a girl, someone sub-perfect, not too threatening, and get rid of your mental baggage. If the opportunity presents itself, unload your virginity. In the grand scheme of things, it doesn't matter who's first, as long as you're happy, and you won't find perfection as long as you insist on looking for it.''

After nine years of a dedicated mind set, it took only about three days to shift gears. I took the next opportunity—a fellow tennis player. She wasn't perfection, but she was what I needed: she was pretty, but not too pretty; she was aggressive (I needed someone else to bust-a-move), but not too aggressive; she was a friend, but not too much of a friend. I just asked her out after a match. We fooled around for a week and that was it.

That brief relationship showed me that I was rustier than I thought. Just before the first time I kissed her, I was terrified, and although the week we spent together was fun, it was relatively awkward nonetheless. I learned that I needed as much ''relationship'' practice as I could get.

Back at college my senior year, I kept my eyes open wider. I changed my approach from ''meet someone, get to know her, become friends, develop the relationship further, start to date, see if she is the woman of my dreams'' to ''fool around first and find out if I like her later.''

The second way was vastly more effective because I didn't have to worry about not being with the ''woman of my dreams'' before I got anywhere sexually. And although the end result was the same, that I would never find the woman of my dreams, at least I had fun and practice in the process.

It was the fall of my senior year at a football game when opportunity knocked. I was in the stands when a woman I had met over the summer recognized me and said hello. We chatted for a moment and I asked her to join up with me later. I saw her at a concert that evening, and after flirting across the room, I asked her out for a drink. We chatted, drank, went back to my off-campus house, up to my room, took off our clothes and went at it. Fifteen seconds (and I'm being generous) after penetration it was over. I lay on top of her and said, "I just lost my virginity." She was shocked and shot me a bewildered stare. "Why me?" she said, "Why me?" From what little she knew of me during our brief interactions over the summer and quick courtship that evening, she couldn't understand why I had chosen her to be my first partner.

After a second round that night (where I was equally as pathetic a lover as in the first session), I lay in bed about to fall asleep and wondered if I would hate myself in the morning. It was ironic that after having spent so long waiting for the perfect partner, I had slept with someone I barely knew. I hadn't cultivated a romantic situation, waiting to do things just so, I had simply jumped into it. I fell asleep trying to draw a conclusion about how it felt to have lost my precious virginity in a way that hadn't matched my earlier fantasy. One thing I decided right away, sex didn't have to be perfect to be fun.

When I woke up the next morning, I was surprised to find that I didn't hate myself. The most overwhelming sensation was that I felt more "normal." I was suddenly more confident and felt little regret. It was as if I had been carrying around all this emotional baggage I thought I needed and had finally thrown it over a cliff and watched it smash and burst open. Out flew the rocks I had been carrying around all that time.

My dad was right! Since I was out of practice and carrying all that baggage, I was terrible, but jumping in gave me confidence to try again and get better. The very best thing of all happened less than six months later. I met the perfect woman, and this time I didn't botch the job. More than seven years later, we are engaged.

Postscript

There was one time less than a year after I lost it when I had my one "true slut" experience. I was in bed with a woman a matter of hours after we met. I call it my "slut" experience because it was clear that neither of us had any intention of forming a relationship; it was just empty and gratuitous sex. I thought it was great. What could be better than sex without obligation? I didn't have to wine and dine or court her for months. What more could I want! A few days later, I started to feel a twinge of pain when I took a leak. Soon, instead of a twinge, it felt like I was pissing fire. I went to the walk-in clinic, where an intern poked and played with my privates, prescribed some drugs, and I began a week's worth of V.D. rehab. It was a drag, but seemed worth it.

Then a year and a bit later, in 1988, AIDS had become just enough of a problem for heterosexuals to catch my attention, and my slut experience became increasingly less worth it. In fact, there was a good long time when I was terrified that I had contracted HIV. I decided to go for a blood test, but because I wasn't in a high risk group, the doctor advised me not to for fear of a false positive diagnosis. It wasn't until a year ago when I gave blood and asked the Red Cross to let me know if I had HIV, that I put my fears to rest. But what a nightmare. In the current environment for sexual disease, even if there is only a remote chance of contracting HIV, it's not even an argument whether or not someone should practice safe sex. The eight seconds of increased pleasure isn't worth the prolonged anxiety and the possibility of death. Back when I was 12, pussy galore was in vogue (then again, so was disco), but now you had better put a helmet on your soldier if you want to lay some pipe.

3

The Wrath of God

by Madeleine Cummings

"Don't ever tell anyone," my mother said, "No one will ever respect you again." I thought of my cousin Lily, condemned as a tramp forever in my mother's mind for her venereal warts, and I kept silent. Mother was right, my disease was God's own punishment for my sin, and I deserved to carry the entire burden alone. Always.

Ten months earlier, I had been a lonely, quirky, 18 year old virgin set loose in Paris, fascinated by medieval history, churches, cathedrals and monasteries. Unlike most young Americans in Paris, I didn't want to dance all night and drink all day. I wanted to come as close as possible to the names I was so familiar with from my readings in history. I remember once stealing a glass from the Cafe de Cluny, simply because it bore the name of an illustrious 10th century monastery. I was not religious, per se, although I had always sung in church choirs, but I had been very enamored of the idea of monastic life: the Rule of St. Benedict intrigued me, and the silence of monasteries, punctuated by liturgical music, drew me.

Despite my innocence and my monastic leanings, my sexual conduct had already been the subject of much discussion back home, culminating in an unpleasant episode when my doctor had decided that at age 18, I should have a pap smear. "Did you tell him anything that would make him think you needed one? You must have!" screamed my mother. I cried and cried, shame being attached even to the very specter of sexual activity. The example of my sister, who had gotten pregnant ten years earlier, and nearly died of an abortion gone septic, was constantly thrown up as an example of what might happen to me if I behaved like a "tramp." Since my sister was largely stigmatized and cast out of the family, the example had a real sting. In my family, sexual activity was equivalent to banishment.

A month after my arrival in Paris, I joined a choir. Halfway through my first rehearsal, the door opened a crack, and a life size, cut-out picture of the popular singer Tino Rossi appeared. Everyone laughed, "Qu'est-ce que c'est que ca?" (Who's that?) and shortly, a tall, jovial, good looking young man appeared. "C'est Thierry! Bien sur!" (Thierry, who else!) I fell in love immediately.

It wasn't long before we were friends, Thierry and I. We were both part of the "young" crowd in the choir, although he was five years older than I. After rehearsals, we'd skip out of the room and down the street, pulling at each others' scarves and jackets, playing those games that now I can recognize as purely sexual, but then, I was innocent of their import.

One Sunday, Thierry invited me to his apartment to taste the Beaujolais Nouveau. We drank it with little bits of sausage, listened to Beethoven's Seventh, and Bob Dylan, and as the wine loosened my inhibitions, I was shocked to hear myself wonder if I would sleep in that double bed of his by the end of my year in Paris. I didn't know it would be so soon.

The next Saturday, we sang together as part of a small ensemble at a wedding. He had a beautiful baritone voice; I was more in love than ever. The playfulness continued: "Let's go kiss the newlyweds!" I laughed at every word, followed his every gesture, and did whatever he suggested.

That night, the choir had a late concert in a rather scary neighborhood. I had never been there so late, and the prostitutes on every corner frightened me. Seeing Thierry as I entered the hall calmed me immediately. "He'll take care of me," I thought, "I'll make sure he walks me to the metro." Thierry had a friend along, and at the end of the concert, the three of us gaily wended our way down the dark streets at nearly midnight. The whores no longer bothered me. I was safe. When we came to the metro, I should have gone in one direction, Thierry and Patrick in another, but no, "kidnapped!" I found myself heading the opposite direction from home, intoxicated by love.

By the time we arrived at Thierry's stop, it was too late to turn back. The last metro had gone. Patrick vanished. I found myself walking up the steps to Thierry's sixth floor apartment, wondering what I was doing there.

"You'll have to spend the night," he said, "do you mind?" "No," I answered brightly, trying to appear far more sophisticated than I felt. I was terrified. Thierry offered me a T-shirt. I crawled into bed, and as he began to kiss me, the flood of conflicting emotions nearly overcame me. I wanted to be loved, to be caressed, to be acknowledged, but at every moment, my mother's voice lingered in my ears, maligning my sister and all "loose" women. How could I even think about sleeping with him? What would become of me?

I pulled myself away. Quavering in my still unpolished French, I found myself telling the long and complicated story of my sister's abortion years before. Thierry listened, nodded soothingly, and began to kiss me again. "C'est interdit de te caresser? Un peu d'amour, quand meme. . . ." (Is it forbidden to caress you? Come on, just a little love.) I had no volition left.

The sexual act itself was painful, but there was only a little blood. Thierry fell asleep afterwards, but I lay awake until dawn. As soon as I thought the first metro would be running, I left. Thierry saw me to the door, singing a corny Christmas carol: "Outside, you're going to be cold, and it's partly my fault." I felt like a stranger to myself.

The pimps and prostitutes of la rue St. Denis were all waiting in that metro for the first train. I felt like I belonged.

Thierry and I slept together once more, that Thursday, and then not ever again, although we continued to see each other at rehearsal, and occasionally outside with other acquaintances from the choir.

I had no friends in Paris with whom I could talk about my experience. I wrote a frantic letter to a friend in the States who was then a freshman in college. While she was as solicitous as she could be at such a distance, she had other concerns, and I still felt tragically alone. My sense of my misbehavior, my misconduct and my sin was present with me through the months. Because Thierry and I had used no contraception, I worried for awhile about getting pregnant. When my period came, I thought I had been pretty lucky.

For a long time, I felt a lingering sense of guilt. I was still in love with Thierry, although our relations were less playful than they had been and that made me extremely unhappy. I felt betrayed, used, and abandoned. I knew I could never tell my family, so I kept up a smile long distance, and talked exclusively about the wonderful new things I was discovering. My phony smile didn't deceive me, however, nor my mother, as it turned out.

In March, I made a long anticipated visit to a living monastic community in a medieval monastery. As I participated in the daily round of monastic life, as I listened to echoes of the Rule of St. Benedict reverberate through every moment of the monastic day, I began to feel drawn not only to the idea of a monastery, but to God. I had never before experienced God in a personal way, as anything other than someone else's idea. But from one moment to another in the cloister as I grasped a slender Gothic pillar, my life changed, and I began to call myself a Christian. God was real to me then, and remains real to me.

And what did God think of my sexual crime? Back in Paris, I cried as I wrote my first letter to the prior of the monastery, telling him of my revelation and asking his advice as to how to proceed. How sinful and unworthy I felt! But that kindly monk assured me of God's grace and love, and encouraged me to return to the monastery. A short while later, I did so, and my visits have continued into the present.

I encountered a very different reception at home in the States. In July, after my return, I went to see a doctor for a physical examination. My mother had pushed me to go, perhaps because she suspected something. I don't think she was altogether surprised to have my pap smear come back positive. That meant I had to see a gynecologist, who informed me I had a fairly severe case of condyloma acuminata, or venereal warts. They were serious enough they could not be removed in the office, and I was going to have to have an operation under general anesthesia. At the time, I remember not really being cognizant that this meant I had certainly been infected by Thierry, and somehow I thought I could have contracted the warts by some other, non-sexual means. This was in fact a possibility, although I didn't learn this until years later. Upon returning from the doctor, I told my mother, who retired to the bedroom, looked up condyloma acuminata in a medical dictionary, and accused me immediately of sleeping around. I no longer remember all the names she called me, or all her insinuations, but I felt as soiled and as dirty as I had ever imagined. For my mother, I had to be either a virgin or a whore.

As her anger flooded over me again and again in the weeks to come, as I felt my sense of shame increase, two points of view began to merge in my mind. Mother, convinced I had betrayed her personally, kept assuring me of my uncleanliness, and I believed at last that there was indeed a God. How much further a step was it to say that this disease was God's punishment for my unforgivable sin?

"Don't ever tell anyone. No one will ever respect you again."

With my mother's insistence on secrecy, I didn't dare write my friends in the monastery, didn't dare tell a single friend from high school, not even the one I had written from Paris, and didn't tell any of my new friends in my freshman dorm. When I had to go into the hospital, I told my professors I had to have a "minor operation" and said nothing to my dorm proctor or advisor. I wrote to Thierry, informing him of my diagnosis. He wrote back a jovial little letter, saying he had known nothing about the warts until just recently. "Fermons la parenthese," he wrote in his offhand way, but for me, the parenthesis was far from closed.

Since my mother was home with cardiac problems, and my father had a business trip, I entered the hospital alone. Even my doctor was a stranger, since my mother had insisted on my continued anonymity, and I was a patient of the public clinic.

Here, indeed, was the Wrath of God. Alone, in a cold and crowded hospital room, with one roommate screaming in pain, another grieving with her husband over her imminent hysterectomy, and a third confessing to her mother over the phone that though she wasn't pregnant, she did have PID, I suffered a great deal in silence. The condescending and inconsiderate manner of my surgeon didn't help. When I asked what she was going to do during the operation, she said she was going to put "medicine" on the warts to make them go away. I wanted to tell her I wasn't a child, but an intelligent woman and deserved to know more about what she was about to do to my body. But my morale was so low I didn't feel worthy of knowing more. God had indeed justly punished me for my lack of willpower. I had sinned, and there were no fruits of joy, or even any solace to be found in sin, only pain, shame, disgrace and silence. God had abandoned me because I was no longer worthy of consideration.

When I reflect back on the utter misery of that time, I marvel at two things—that I was ever able to love God again, and that I slept with anyone afterwards, the shame and the imagined disgrace hurt me so deeply. I owe the first to the monastic community that had welcomed me in the month of March, who continued over the years to impress me with the power of God's love, and not his avenging wrath; and I owe the second to falling in love in the sexually casual atmosphere of a college dorm. The feeling of dirtiness, however, lived on for years.

For a long time, my medical records were incomplete, lacking any mention of my operation, since my mother had insisted I not have the records transferred from the big city hospital where I had been operated on out of fear that the story would somehow "come out." Even when later, as a part of a physical examination, I decided to tell my physician, I felt ashamed and was afraid she would judge me as severely as had my mother, and, it seemed, God.

It is only now, nine years later, that I have been able to tell this story without shame. When I told a lover recently, he wept with me, and it is perhaps in those tears, which contained no blame and no shame, that I have been able to put to rest the myth of the wrath of God. It is not God who punishes us for sexual misconduct, but we ourselves and those around us who turn what may well be deserved regret into unfounded and unkind disgrace.

Losing one's virginity shouldn't be a capital crime, and those who are as unlucky as I shouldn't be made to feel that venereal disease is in any way a punishment from Heaven for their "misconduct." Certainly, I now regret having slept with Thierry, but I no longer believe that God wreaked a terrible vengeance on me through venereal disease. That vengeance came instead from my mother, who could not accept her daughter's sexual activity, and chose to treat me like a puppy, pushing my nose again and again into my mistake, to see if shame would somehow cure me of my evil habits.

I find it difficult, even now, to forgive my mother entirely. My shame may have vanished, but the remembered sense of it, the memory of the tears I shed, the unhappiness and especially the loneliness she drove me to, has not. That she should have led me to mistake my misfortune for the wrath of God is also hard to forgive, for it combined earthly discomfort with divine retribution. I would not like to see the same fate fall to anyone.

4

Batman, Hot Dogs and the Ultimate Zucchini

by Chris Fischer

My last girlfriend leaked me some very, very sensitive feminine information. We were basking in the warmth of a midspring's eve, she contemplating the cosmos and I contemplating her navel, when it just popped out. The sensitive information, I mean. When she and her friends were first discovering the joys of masturbation, she said, the penis-substitute of choice was often, well, a zucchini. And this was in *Iowa*.

After I stopped laughing, I started thinking.

Thought #1: How honored I am, as a 27-year-old male, to have been leaked such sensitive feminine information, etc., etc.

Thought #2: A zucchini? Thank God I didn't grow up in Iowa, whose male population grew up listening to a feminine chorus of "You mean it doesn't get any bigger?"

Thought #3: This topic makes me horny. So we did it. Like, um uh, vegetables, I guess. (The reason we broke up was not zucchini-related.)

I haven't forgotten that startling revelation and have since revised my conception of sexual maturity. I have decided that I never "lost" my "virginity" when I was a teenager.

No, I didn't lose my virginity in a dark dorm room one night during my first semester at college with a girl named Wendy from Holyoke who was wearing candy-striped panties. Not that she wasn't the first woman with whom I'd ever fornicated. She was. She was also kind and gentle and sweet and had a swimmer's body that sucked me dry in no time flat.

No, that's not why. See, I never really had my "virginity" to begin with.

* * *

The zippered fly in my soup is that the word *virginity* just doesn't turn me on. Creaking under centuries of religious taboo and repressed randiness, *virginity* has staggered into the 90s implying an improbable "purity" whose loss is to be regretted or not regretted, as the case may be. This goes double or more for women, who have had to bear the weight of their husband's double standards—and, due to the missionary position's general popularity among men, their husbands. And we're just talking heterosexuality here.

I prefer a different spin: that when I was growing up in that small, suburban New England town o' mine, I lost my ignorance, not my innocence. I learned how to please my body while pleasing others'. Sure, achieving "zucchini" status was a significant goal of sorts. For heterosexuals it was the real thing, the Big Time, the thing that could get girls knocked up if you weren't careful. It was fun to celebrate. It was also the most socially accepted sexual milestone. People didn't go around saying "Check it out! I lost my anal virginity last night!" If you did somebody up the wazoo, it didn't count.

But by the time Wendy came along to cement my hetero leanings, I was well down the road to a goal far more worthy than simply getting laid or otherwise conforming to somebody else's hazy idea of "manhood." That's right: I was on the road to becoming the Ultimate Zucchini. And I still am.

* * *

Okay. It's coming back now. Ummmmmmmmmmm.

I can remember a warm fire in a darkened dorm room, Simon and Garfunkel oozing from an old Emerson tape deck; my first embarrassing tango with a condom, which I ran out of the bedroom to put on; her new panties, cotton and striped like a melted candy cane.

After the act I remember thinking something along the lines of "Wow—now I'm a man!" I felt like a Manx cat that suddenly finds itself with a full tail. (Fortunately, she wasn't from Iowa.) And I remember asking Wendy, as she was now giving me a bedroom backrub, "Were you a . . . I mean, was this your . . . ?"

Like the hands that paused briefly on my lumbar vertebrae, her reply was gentle but firm. "Nope. You?"

"Er—Yep," I said.

Aye, but here's the bedroom rub: I could have said, "Well, it's certainly not the first time I've come across a friendly orifice."

For, in all truth, it wasn't. Like most budding heteros, I was *de facto* homo long before any zucchini-hungry vaginas came my way. Then, when the time came (and the candy-cane panties came off), I made the switch. That's all.

I surfed over adolescence like Batman surfing off a shark-infested coastline in one of those episodes that had me glued to the TV four hours a day. I didn't get involved in all the cliques, hazing, back-biting and other crap that turns other people's middle- and high-school years into Dante's *Inferno* with Varsity letters. Instead, I whipped shark repellent out of my Bat-belt and sprayed it at people until they left me alone. Then I got braces, which did the job automatically.

There was just one problem: hormones.

Life was a permanent hard-on. I had a hard-on when I got up in the morning, a hard-on on the school bus, a hard-on in Algebra—pretty much every time I sat still for a few minutes. My English classes taught me about Man vs. Nature, and I figured this was one battle Man always lost. My Bat-cape cloaked a raging boner. Life was hard, indeed.

When we weren't wetting our beds, my friend Tom and I blew up condoms and batted them around in his backyard, developing motor skills that would serve us well in college. Neither of us was a locker-room athlete, though, so our vocabulary was pretty limited.

At one point a fifth-grade friend and I would float twig boats down the brook by the house one minute and the next flip a huge, fake buffalo nickel for photographs of naked women cut from "Penthouse," "Playboy" and "Hustler" and whatever else we could get our grubby little paws on. If girls objectified us boys as zucchinis, we soon learned to objectify them as, well, zucchini receptacles.

I rifled my Dad's sock drawer and bedside stand regularly, although to his credit I rarely found much (my brother's closet collection was much more dependable). And when I joined the Boy Scouts, I found that my happy-camper colleagues, when they weren't learning to be brave, clean and reverent, were amassing huge collections of glossy smut. (My sister, bless her soul, finally gave me a book on sex written for teens. "Great," I thought, "but where are the pictures?"

As any pervert will tell you, this wasn't a cause, but a symptom of our sexual obsession. One day after high school, I stopped by my friend Scott's house to shoot some hoops. (He wasn't into Trojan balloonery; maybe that's why he's an ordained minister now). When we went inside for a drink, the family dachshund attacked my leg—not to bite it, but to hump it for all he was worth. Scott laughed, and told me that Fred humped pretty much anything that moved.

I looked at Fred, and Fred looked at me. We definitely had something in common; for us it was a constant.

"Down, Fred," I said.

* * *

Despite the shark repellent, my sexual landscape finally began acquiring some features when I got to high school. Even for this skinny dweeb there were a few feel-up sessions with high school girls giving freely of their upper torsos, at least. I owe it all to music. There was Michelle the flute player on her living room sofa; Daven the marching-band majorette on my living room sofa; Laura the musical-actress in the car after the cast party, and again after a flick ("Risky Business," as I recall). And dearest Mindy, my only real "girlfriend" before college.

But here's where I parted company with the jocks, freaks, and others who formed the party circuit. I just didn't party. I wasn't a Bored Teen, even if you didn't count masturbation.

But even with Mindy I didn't go "all the way," didn't "hit a home run." She played viola, piano, and harp, but didn't play me. She just wasn't into it yet, and I wasn't the type to press the issue.

So apart from dressing up like a zucchini, what was a boy to do but, but . . . practice? Mike showed me how he masturbated. Steve and I jerked off together. Eddie first went down on me. And finally, up the butt we all went. Like Fred the dick-brained dachshund, the frustrated little boys of suburbia ran to each other, putting the *homo* back in *homo sapiens*. Unlike Fred, we were picking on someone our own size, and our prey was as horny as he.

For those of us who were discovering their true homosexuality, it was epiphany. For the rest, it was sexual R & D. It was sex by proxy, vicarious sex, good-enough-for-rock-&-roll sex. It was sex to destroy any later political career. It was great. Though we still had no idea what girls liked, this proto-zucchini stuff was fun. Guilty fun, but fun.

My first time up the Hershey Highway must have been with my balloon-blowing buddy Tom. I say "must have been" because I don't even remember the first time. For me the whole thing was an undressed dress rehearsal, the next best thing to actually making it with that gorgeous high-school senior populating my daydreams. Tom fantasized about Liz, I fantasized about—uh, whatever her name was—and we had a ball. As it were.

But I knew the terrifying consequences of revealing as much to my homophobic classmates. I kept it close to my hairless chest, surfing away from anyone who came close to the truth. Like my fellow sexual initiates, I thought it better to be hypocritical than sorry. "Gayness" was so associated with wrongness that "don't be gay" meant "don't be a jerk." Meanwhile, all us real jerks were jerking each other off in secret. Mentally or physically, none of us, certainly, was a "virgin" by any stretch of the condom—I mean, imagination.

* * *

Of course, all this proto-sex wasn't that terrific. I'm still making up for all those parties I missed, all the hetero hanky-panky I hid from behind my mask and cape. Since that darkened college dormroom, I've had the great privilege of doing it in hot tubs, in a bathroom, in cars, in a pool, in a frenzy, in Philadelphia, in broad daylight, ineptly, indubitably, ineffably, indescribably, in her own sweet time. Though I've often felt like Fred, I've been able to refine my instincts somewhat. Like Fred with blinders, maybe.

But the fact remains that I have not come much closer to Ultimate Zucchinidom than I was ten years ago. Mostly what I've done is make lust. Occasionally I've made like. I've even made infatuated-by; and it's often been extremely intense. But I've never truly, madly, deeply made "love." To me, this—not some cockamamie vision of sexual chastity—constitutes a lack of purity, of "virginity." You don't lose the sucker, you *gain* it.

I haven't thought much about this. I like surprises too much to really iron it out. I know it has something to do with relinquishing personal autonomy, allowing myself to need somebody, that kind of thing. And I imagine it means settling down with a mate, at last enjoying the thrill of actually *trying* to get someone pregnant. You know, deciding to do the fambly thang, joining society for real.

It could just possibly make for great sex, too. Boredom? Pah! Boredom comes when our imaginations just can't get it up. That shouldn't happen to me until I'm well into my second mortgage.

But if you'll excuse me, I think I'll put maturity off for a rainy day in the future, like when I feel like staying in one place for longer than a year. I mean, in the days before health care and pensions and social safety nets, only the horniest survived—only the Freds of the world, who went forth and multiplied. Now, though, there are too gosh-darn many of us *homo sapiens* around for our own good. It's about time more of us took the hint and just enjoyed sex for what it is.

Yes, I can vaguely make out the Ultimate Zucchini down there at the end of my road. I might as well take my time, and enj—heeeey, hey ho honeypie, didn't expect to see *you* here! Looking for spring veggies, I see? Va va va voom, look no further. . . .

5

Boys Will Be Boys

by Braxton Brittle

The mattress on the downstairs pullout couch had met with a great deal of general abuse. Friends would come over and we'd turn the couch into a bed so we could all fit uncomfortably on top of each other. It was the battleground for many pillow fights, wrestling matches, and trampoline exhibitions. It was the site of the annual 'Sweat and Snore'—a gathering of friends marked by eating, drinking, and laughing until sunrise whereupon we all flopped on the bed sweating from the intense body heat my friend Michele vented and listening to my friend Sue snoring. We beat up on it mercilessly.

It was no surprise then that a severe valley had formed down the center of the pullout. My friends and I had broken the spine of this pullout to the point where anyone on it gradually yet eventually ended up sliding into the mattress' center of gravity. It was like trying to sleep or sit on a very wide sliding board. We loved it.

This pullout is where I first experienced the big one. It was the summer preceding junior year of high school and I had never been touched there before. I couldn't believe how much better it was when someone else was doing it to you. I was only wearing my briefs and the feeling of a hand moving in between my legs was debilitating and strange.

We were both vying for space in the gully of the bed. An elbow in my ear. My thumb up a nostril. General thrashing as we tried to find the jigsaw fit that would allow both of us a comfortable position in which to slumber. The dampness of the basement made wet those patches of skin where our bodies met. The blanket had been pulled up over both of us making that wetness warm and slippery rather than cool and clammy. Then I felt his fingers touching me.

Our bodies pressed together. The hand moved gently and purposely with a metronomic rhythm. I feigned sleep. "Breathe," I kept telling myself. Breathe in, breathe out. In and out. I tried to think about how people look on television when they breathe in their sleep. How they sound. Sleep breathing. Back and forth the hand kept moving.

I shivered when I felt warm breath on my neck; the hand stopped for a moment and then reconvened its dutiful movement. I'd never been touched like this by another person. I liked it. More than anything I wanted him to kiss me so that I might kiss him back. I wanted him to know that I liked it. I didn't make a move even though I was dying to; all I did was think "breathe" and "sleep." I was lying on my stomach for the most part and the erection I had gotten was awkwardly stuck in my briefs and being crushed by the weight of my own body. The situation needed fixin'—I thought permanent damage was being done. I had to move.

In an Academy-award winning performance, I grumbled, and in what I wanted to be perceived as a sleepy fit, turned onto my back. He was naked. With slow methodic pulls, he took off my briefs. The clothing tension was dissipated and I lay perfectly still. I thought, "Now is the perfect opportunity for him to kiss me." "Do it now," I noiselessly implored. But the kiss remained absent.

And then he started to really touch me. He was running his hand over my chest and my erection. He guided one of my hands along the length of his body to do the same and I did so faithfully. Not only had I never been touched like this before, but I also had never been presented with the opportunity to explore, probe, touch, and caress someone else.

Steve was in control. He had hegemony over me in a fundamental sense. A total exploration of each other's bodies transpired. He could make me tense up with every touch. He had cleared his throat. I knew he was awake, he had cleared his throat. Had I given it away yet? Did he think I was still asleep? I mumbled the name "Lisa" and emitted soft groans.

But I can't imagine he actually believed I was still asleep. Every time he would breathe on my ear, I would arch my back which just encouraged his hands to work more quickly. Moreover, I was jerking him off. With the same cadence he was using on me, I methodically rubbed my hand up and down him. Sleepwalking is one thing, but this was quite something else. His soft groans also told me he was awake and encouraged me to continue. And I did. Nary a word was spoken.

It's important to point out that I was having a great time. This was good stuff. I figured this is what "hot, sweaty sex" was; and I was psyched. I could feel both myself and him getting more and more excited. And this was definitely better than making out with my girlfriend under the bleachers at school had ever been.

"Blow me." Is that what he mumbled? "Blow me." Again. A whisper. He was moving himself out of the bed's valley. I could feel him kneeling beside me. He couldn't have been asleep. There was no way. My eyes had been closed this entire time and I kept them closed. Breathe in. Out. A leg was lifted over my head. He was straddling me and I didn't know what to do. I felt my head in between his legs and then he opened my mouth with a finger. Breathe. I closed my eyes tighter as he put himself inside.

"Blow me." At first, I blew. I had no clue. But then it became obvious what I was supposed to do when he lay down on top of me. I felt his tongue doing to me what he wanted done to him. Mercy. I opened my eyes for the first time and while staring up at the ceiling through his legs, I tried to figure out what I was going to do about this thing in my mouth. Was this petting? "Oh my God," I thought, "this is petting." He did something that made me convulse and he drew back immediately. But he started up again and I blindly and mechanically mimicked his oral actions.

After a few moments, he was, as it were, making me crazy. I couldn't place what was happening to me in any experiential context. This intense, passionate state in which I had no capability for thinking took me over. I had grabbed hold of him tightly and my toes were extended. He switched back to his hand and I had my first non-self-induced orgasm.

Steve immediately got up off of me, I still feigned sleep. He went into the bathroom next to the bed. I got up and listened at the door. He was taking care of himself. Why hadn't he let me do that. Had I wanted to? I got back in bed, still messy, still naked, shivering from the cold air.

He woke me up. "Hey, Jonathan, look what you've done. You kept saying 'Lisa.' Clean yourself up. What was she doing to you in that dream that made you cream so bad?" He had put on his shorts and a T-shirt.

It was only a few minutes later that I climbed back in the pullout bed and under the sheets. I also had shorts and a T-shirt on. His back was toward me. He rested on the edge of his side of the bed. After what seemed several hours, I was still awake, but breathing as though I weren't. In and out. In and out. I wanted to kiss him. Just once on his face. "Please let me kiss you goodnight." I reached over and gingerly let my hand light on his back. He shook it off. I replaced it on his shoulder blade. He slapped it away.

I tried again after what seemed like another hour. Another shove away.

I held my hand in the air for a moment, not sure what to do with it. I put it down on the bed in between my body and his—flat and spread out. I was covered by a blanket, but shaking nonetheless. It had been warmer when our legs had been intertwined. I had felt extremely close to Steve sleeping pressed up against him. Rolling over, I pulled my knees up near my chest and wrapped my arms around my legs. I looked over my shoulder across the bed and the small canyon in the center—I could barely recognize what was on the other side. I shoved my face down into my pillow and fell asleep that night clinging to the outer edge of my side of the bed.

Nothing was ever said. Steve and I never duplicated the encounter. I never even hinted to him that I hadn't been asleep or that I knew about what we had done. But every time that we were together I wanted it to happen again. I knew that I wasn't going to be able to get anyone else to interact with me like that for a while. I started to think of Steve constantly. I obsessed over him even more.

The obsession with Steve wasn't anything new. Everybody liked Steve. To me, he seemed perfect. He was attractive, athletic, funny, and popular. He flirted well with all the girls, and he knew how to act cool. We were classmates in high school and involved in a bunch of the same activities. We initiated staying over at each other's houses and sleeping in the same bed when another classmate of ours hanged himself. I think that my mother was worried about my reaction and asked Steve's mother if I might stay with their family while mine went away. It was during marching band camp that summer that we started to hang together. Maybe it was the invariably ridiculous process of maneuvering seventy, basically indifferent high school students about a football field into complex formations for the benefit of a student body who thought that we were all losers that made us closer. Maybe he could tell that I doted on him and he liked that. Maybe we were truly becoming friends.

I wanted to be just like Steve. I was well-liked, but not popular. I was brainy and not quite in tune with what it took to be "hip" and "cool." I adored him. I attempted to emulate him. I was thrilled when our friendship took off. I looked up to him and often found myself studying him. I remember talking to him on the phone and demanding that he recount his day to me verbatim—I wanted and needed to account for every minute of his time away from me. How many times had I called his house to see if he was there or not? How many times had I hung up when someone else answered?

So, the obsession was nothing new. But it had gained new fire. For two more years of high school, I would see him every day. We traveled in some of the same social circles. I tried to befriend all of his friends and especially his girlfriends. I'd sit and stare at him. Could he possibly have done all that in his sleep? Does he remember? Do he and his other friends do that sort of thing all the time? Should I mention that night to him? Why can't it happen again? Didn't he enjoy it? Maybe I did something wrong. What had happened? Did he understand what had happened? Is he gay? Does he think I'm gay? Has he told anyone about it? It became clear that I was hopelessly attracted to him. I wanted it to happen again. Even though we grew apart (partly because of the sexual encounter I'm sure) I always thought about him.

Indeed, I was confused. Admitting to yourself that you're gay can be a daunting task let alone while you're still in high school. I never asked Steve any of the questions over which I often agonized. I never told anyone. I kept it all inside.

In college I learned in an adolescent development class that approximately fifty percent of all boys between the ages of twelve and seventeen have some sort of same-sex intimate experience. This knowledge made me feel like I might not be quite such a freak after all. But by that time, I was beginning to realize I was not attracted to women, but to men. And it was not until I entered law school, nearly seven years after Steve gave me my first burrito (as it were) that I effectively dealt with and came to grips with being gay. During the interim I had girlfriends and sexual intercourse with several of them, but I could tell something wasn't right and I knew I'd never be happy if I continued dating women. I realized my attraction to men was not something I was capable of changing. It is not a sexual preference, it's a sexual orientation.

Coming out to myself as well as to my friends and family finally enabled me to stop worrying about what was "wrong" with me. I was happy. I had provided myself with an avenue for being happy. There was nothing wrong with me at all. The wrong exists in a society that rejects and beats up on being gay, which makes it very easy for such individuals to repress who they really are and deny their sexuality to themselves. I was scared of what would happen if I dared to say "I'm gay." Would I get the proverbial hairy palms? Would I spontaneously combust? Would a large inverted pink triangle suddenly appear on all my clothes trumpeting to the world that I date men and not women? My fears proved false; a large part of my life that was in disarray was now manageable.

I think Steve's experience of our intimate encounter was homosexual and not gay. And it's extremely important to address the difference. For

Steve, I believe it was adolescent concupiscence manifesting itself; for me, it was something more. A good example can be drawn from what currently takes place in many of America's penal correctional institutions. Male inmates often perform homosexual acts with each other, but that does not make them gay. A homosexual act does not make a gay person. Some of these inmates choose to engage in same-sex relations because of the specific circumstances in which they find themselves, not because they are emotionally and physically attracted to men instead of women. Gay is not an option or a preference, it is a way of being. I'm often asked by straight people "What makes you gay?" The best response I've come up with is "The same thing that makes you not gay."

I choose to be called gay. I prefer not to be labelled a homosexual. "Homosexual," carries a sterile, scientific connotation. The word focuses on the act of sex: sex between two who are alike. The gestalt of gay, the components of desire, love, and sensitivity necessary in any relationship, are usurped by the term homosexual. This problem also exacerbates the perception that much of society seems to have that gay people are lust-driven, crazed, sex monkeys, incapable of long-term relationships or marriage-like commitment. The term homosexual puts all the emphasis on the physical aspect of a relationship and doesn't include the concomitant mental and emotional states that gay people (like straight people) experience when they are involved with someone and in love.

Many of the feelings I had for Steve as my peer idol were intensified that night in my basement. The experience with Steve was a gay experience for me even though I couldn't clearly identify or label the emotions that Steve had elicited from me. I didn't even know that I was gay or what the word meant. The terms "fag" and "queer" were thrown around liberally in high school, but they had no meaning for me. I couldn't relate to the idea that two men could love each other. No one pointed out that there were other kinds of possibilities. I thought I was a freak.

I lost my virginity with Steve that night. I had the first sexual experience of my life, but my first sexual experience "after" realizing and admitting to myself that I was gay was like losing my virginity entirely anew. Unlike my passive and confused state with Steve, this time I was mentally and physically engaged in what was going on. I wasn't very experienced; what mattered was that this time I was there as a whole person.

I met John at a coffee house on campus. We were both with other friends, but the two groups merged and John and I sat next to each other. I was attracted to him physically from the outset and after talking to him for a while, I started to fall for him. He was a graduate student in a Ph.D program at the university. He was smart, funny, quick-witted, charming, and laughed at my jokes. I felt like Prince Charming had just walked into my life. We spoke until the coffee house closed and I excused myself to go and do some reading for law school.

The next day I called up one of my friends who had been present the night before in order to do some research. My friend answered the phone and when he heard my voice, said, "I'm surprised you didn't give me my wake up call. You want to know about John, don't you?" Neither of us had been very subtle, but there had been no need to be. He was available, sensitive, and from everything my friend could tell, ready to meet someone new. I wasted no time and gave John a call on the pretense of not having a running partner for the afternoon and did he want to accompany me. He couldn't, but dinner plans were made.

The next two weeks of dating were frustrating, fun, and full of self-doubt. Fun because we had a great time together. Frustrating because I didn't know how he felt about me. We were spending large chunks of time together and if we didn't see each other, we at least spoke every day. We had kissed once, but I was totally flummoxed and couldn't remember how it had gone. I was full of self-doubt because I was afraid there was something wrong with me and that my appearance wasn't making him fall for me. I looked in the mirror every opportunity I had.

One Thursday night, we had a movie date and then he was supposed to come over and watch "L.A. Law" in my room. During the movie, we held hands, fooled around, and giggled. For the first time, I could tell that genuine mutual attraction existed. We returned to my room and as he opened the bottle of wine he had brought, I kissed him.

We never saw "L.A. Law" that night. For several hours, we did nothing but kiss and hug. The greatest pleasure came from the sense of security that accompanied being held so closely and tightly by John. Some time after midnight, it seemed that we both simultaneously decided that in order to be even closer we would have to remove some clothing and we began to undress each other. All fears about my appearance had vanished. I remember the incredible excitement that went with him putting my legs over his shoulders and removing my pants. I sighed with relief. I couldn't wait to touch him and I couldn't wait for him to touch me. I knew what was going on and that it was what I wanted to happen.

We had sex that night. There was oral sex and mutual masturbation. I reveal these intimate details because it's important to point out that not all gay sex is anal sex. In fact, gay sex may never include anal sex of any kind. I am neither a pitcher nor a catcher, neither a fudge-packer nor a pillow-biter. I don't participate in anal sex. It's a personal choice in gay sex just as it is a personal choice in straight sex. I would be lying if I claimed that avoiding anal sex had nothing to do with a fear of AIDS and the HIV virus. (I don't deny the possibility of exposure to the HIV virus during oral sex.) In many ways, I've come to associate sex with death. The reasons, however, go beyond this apprehension and to a basic lack of desire to participate in that particular form of intercourse.

John and I fell asleep entwined. My eyes opened in the morning before his, and I lay still listening to his breathing. I watched his face and chest move up and down and felt an overwhelming sense of affection and safety. He eventually woke up to find me looking straight down into his eyes. We spent that morning in bed in silence and that was fine. I kept thinking that I wanted to tell John that I loved him, but something held me back. I didn't want to scare him away and wasn't even sure that love was what I was feeling. I'd certainly never had such good sex before. I'd never connected intimately that well with someone. Maybe I was mistaking lust, the novelty of the relationship, and wanting to be in love with someone for the real thing. I kept quiet. I was content with John wrapped around me. The need to go to class finally broke up our morning vigil.

Losing it this time around was much better than losing it the first time.

I'm no longer with John even though our relationship was good, healthy, and my longest-lasting to date. It ended when we were no longer on campus together. But I think about John often and still wonder whether I was in love with him. I still like John and when I recall our time together my thoughts of him are positive and warm. Steve is a different story. When I think about Steve, images of a large cyst growing hair and teeth pop into my mind. In retrospect, seven years later, I feel like I was used. I cringe when I entertain the notion that I considered him one of my best friends and wanted to be just like him. He made me feel dispensable and inadequate. When I think of our incident together, even now, those feelings flow back vivid and strong.

Reconciling the intense physical pleasure of losing my virginity with the awful emotional baggage the experience carried with it was a difficult task for a high school student who felt he could talk to no one about the incident. It was very hard to figure whether what I felt emanated from the heart or from a physical sensation or both. It was my first experience and was with a person I painstakingly adored. Did I love Steve? What he did to me that night made me think that I did. Did I love him because I did or because he had touched me like that?

Much later with John when I was much more aware of myself, I was still unable to separate the physical from the emotional. Why had I wanted to tell John that I loved him? The two were still blurred. When I muse about what I'd like to hear, however, things somewhat come into focus. After all, I'd like someone to tell me that they love me at times other than only when we are in bed together. If I conclude that I could be guilty of doing just that, then I know my attachment is shallow or waning. In high school, the onslaught of puberty and passion rendered lame my ability to figure this out and think about it rationally. The only excuse I have is to declare that love and emotions aren't rational.

I know that I'll see both John and Steve again, and I can predict how I'll feel about being around each one. Both of them have had profound influences over me that would probably be news to them. Both gave me insight into what sex and intimacy could and would be like. One I will always cherish for showing me what wonderful things are possible; the other I will put away behind a closed door to remind me that the self-deprecating, self-denying tendencies I felt after being with him are really the only things that belong in a closet.

6

Performance: What's Likely to Happen

by Dennis M. Dailey, D.S.W., Professor
The University of Kansas School of Social Welfare

Before I begin, you need to know where I am coming from. I operate on the assumption that every human being is a sexual human being from the moment of birth to the moment of death. We are born sexual human beings. That accounts for why little children (and most adults also) enjoy fondling their genitals, because it feels so darn good. It also accounts for why a lot of older adults (your parents and grandparents) enjoy their sexual interactions, because it feels so darn good and it is important to their relationships. And a lot of older adults are having much better sex than younger people; they have had a lot more practice.

We do not have a choice about whether we are sexual human beings or not. We only have choices about the expression of our sexuality: why, when, where, with whom, how, etc. and like your parents, most of you are not likely to check it out with your parents before you have sexual experiences. Your parents did not check it out with their parents either.

Here is the bottom line for me. If and when you choose to express your sexuality, I hope that experience is an unbelievably, memorably, fantastically pleasurable experience physically, emotionally and relationally. I do not want your choice to express your sexuality to be burdened by things like guilt and shame, unwanted pregnancy, STDs, coercion, inability to have orgasm, ejaculating too quickly, lack of sexual desire, erectile problems, etc. Who needs these outcomes!

Although important, it is not enough to know things that will reduce the hurt, like how to use condoms and other contraceptives, how to make decisions consistent with your own beliefs and values, or how to avoid pressure to be who you are not. You also need to know lots of things about how to insure that your sexual interactions are really pleasurable and meaningful. I can guarantee that pleasure is not automatic. For example, in first experiences with sexual interaction almost all men experience ejaculation and orgasm, yet very few women experience orgasm. Why is that? It is because men do not understand very much about female sexuality (or their own for that matter) and neither do a lot of women. Thus, women cannot tell men what they want and need and most men do not have a clue. Another example. Lots of men in their first experiences with sexual intercourse, ejaculate or "come" very quickly; a few seconds is not uncommon. Why is that? It is because young men are so anxious about doing well that the anxiety overpowers their ability to gain some voluntary control over what is essentially an involuntary reflex. So they "come" quickly. If you are into speed that would be OK, but a few seconds seems a bit fast. Right?!

Now, about performance. Sexual interactions, whether it be sexual intercourse or all of those other sexual interactions that are so erotically pleasurable, are not performances. Yet, that is exactly what they so often turn out to be, especially in our first experiences of expressing our sexuality. And the performance standards are so off-the-graph unrealistic and surrounded in mythology. Here are some of the performance standards and demands that we bring to sexual interactions that get in the way of them being pleasurable and meaningful and increase the likelihood of hurt, especially if we lack sexuality education that is honest, full and real.

MYTH: Men are supposed to last a long time before they come and definitely last long enough to "give" a woman an orgasm.

COMMENT: The average male will last between 3 and 5 minutes in active penal/vaginal intercourse. Only in the fantasy letters in "Penthouse" do men last for hours. Besides, most women are definitely not looking forward to an hour of sexual intercourse. Three to five minutes is just fine, thank you. Also, men do not give women orgasms. No man alive has ever done that. Women are in charge of their own orgasms and will have them when they are ready, if they have learned to have orgasms. Also, only about a fourth of women have orgasms during sexual intercourse with any reliability. Intercourse does not provide the kind of stimulation most women need in order to achieve orgasm. Yet almost three-fourths of women learn how to have orgasms, but they find other, more effective ways of achieving them.

MYTH: Women are supposed to have orgasms every time they are sexually expressive, especially during intercourse, and preferably they should have multiple orgasms.

COMMENT: See above. But more importantly, women must know what they need and want and then facilitate it in their sexual interactions. That means women will have to know their own bodies and how they work and they will have to be comfortable with their own bodies. Most women who have orgasms learn to give them to themselves first, then they share them with a lover. It is true that women have the capacity for multiple orgasms, but they are not a requirement for satisfaction.

MYTH: If you have had sexual intercourse, then you have experienced intimacy.

COMMENT: Sexual intercourse means you have experienced physical closeness. Intimacy requires the expression of emotions, usually verbally. It means risking feelings with others and having those feelings returned when possible. Many sexual experiences are devoid of intimacy.

MYTH: Here is a really deadly one. Perfect sex, doing it right, meeting the ideal standard requires that two people, involved in sexual intercourse only, both come and do so at exactly the same time.

COMMENT: Good luck! That is pretty unusual, except that everyone is secretly working to meet that standard. Work and pressure to perform will definitely get in the way of a pleasurable/meaningful sexual interaction. There is a powerful assumption that sexual intercourse is the only and best sexual experience. Who can deny that it is fun and pleasurable? But there are so many other experiences that can be erotic and need to be incorporated into sexual interactions. The expectation of the simultaneous, mutual orgasm is really undermining to so many sexual interactions.

MYTH: If you have sexual intercourse, then you are a sexual person.

COMMENT: Wrong! You were born sexual, you will die sexual. Having sexual intercourse means you have expressed your sexuality through sexual intercourse. Most people express their sexuality well before they have sexual intercourse. Sex does not equal intercourse, and intercourse does not equal sex.

MYTH: Men are supposed to have large penises (8 to 12 inches would be good) because men believe: 1) Big penises give women big orgasms, 2) Women love big penises, and 3) Big penises make you a big man.

COMMENT: Wrong! The size of a man's penis has very little to do with a woman's pleasure. Women are much more concerned about the man who is connected to the penis, whether he cares about her or is just using her, whether he knows how to use his penis, and whether he has all of his self-esteem wrapped up in what he does with his penis. Not only do women not particularly care about the size of a man's penis, the large ones (there are a few out there, but not many) scare the hell out of them. It is only in the "Penthouse" fantasies that all of the men seem to have 8, 10, 12 inch penises. The vast majority of men all end up with erect penises that are about 6 inches long, plus or minus about a half inch. That is just fine, unless you are into pole vaulting.

MYTH: If you have sexual intercourse it will prove that he/she loves you.

COMMENT: Having sexual intercourse means you have had sexual intercourse. If sexual intercourse always meant "I love you," lots of men would not dump women after they have had sexual intercourse. Having sexual intercourse also will not repair a relationship that has gone sour.

Well, these are just a few of the performance demands that many young people bring to their sexual interactions, and every one of them will detract from the pleasure, if your goal is to meet or exceed those standards. To be honest, lots of people labor under these expectations, even most parents. And they have the same consequence in marriage. Maybe that attitude has something to do with all of the failed marriages in our society (50%).

Like I said, sexual expression is not a performance. It is a mutually shared experience of enjoying the fullness of a physical and emotional relationship with others. Women do not look forward to being performed on; they look forward to a shared experience of caring, which is also true for a lot of men (we are not only interested in one thing). Men obsessed with performance always feel like failures and never feel the fullness of the pleasure and meaningfulness of sexual interactions. Women pressing themselves to have orgasms almost never have them. Women concerned about having a perfect body (there are not many perfect bodies) are distracted from the pleasure of their own bodies. Women expecting men to give them an orgasm are definitely in trouble, and so many women end up faking orgasms to make men feel good. They are certainly not doing it for their pleasure.

Sexual interactions are not performances, I repeat. Sexual interactions are opportunities to express caring, love, closeness and maybe commitment, in physical interaction with others. Sexual interactions are supposed to be pleasurable and meaningful, not hurtful and scary. So, when you choose, and I do hope it is a choice to be sexually expressive (lots of women are coerced and raped), I hope you know enough to make that experience pleasurable and that you know enough to avoid the hurt that can occur. It is not supposed to hurt in any way, physically or emotionally.

7

Love in Black and White

by Nancy Brown

My first experience making love was a wonderful, slow, gentle, gradual process. My boyfriend and I were both dizzy with love. Indeed, he used to comment that he felt high after kissing me. The experience was new and warm.

I grew up in a rural Maine community; our family led the perfect alternative life style. My picturesque childhood instilled old fashioned values in me. I expected to marry the first man I made love with, however, I was modern enough to realize I would most likely experience sex before marriage. Abstaining from premarital sex certainly seems as outdated as Elvis and bobby socks even though AIDS may bring abstinence back in style.

I was the most old-fashioned person, sexually speaking, of all my friends. I simply did not belong to the school of thought that a woman owes a man a sexual favor in return for an evening on the town even though many men feel cheated when they do not receive "a return on their investment."

In my mind, one has sex with the person one is in love with. That is why it's called making love. I believe that love takes a very long time to develop. At the age of fifteen or sixteen, a person is not capable of understanding love and all the consequences and responsibilities tied up in the sexual package.

Most of my high school friends were having sex. My best friend and I were the only exceptions. I was always the last to know who had just "done it" and with whom. My friends would confide in my best friend, and she would give me the latest gossip. They were scared to tell me directly because they knew how outspoken I was on the subject and felt I would disapprove of their behavior.

To be honest, I had little sympathy for my friends who were emotionally hurt by their first experience. I believed they should have known better. Bottom line: guys will do or say anything for a little pussy. Many of my friends were used their first time. Their experiences were usually harsh, rough, quick and uncommunicative, performed in the back seats of cold cars parked down old dirt roads late at night, or in damp unheated summer camps late in March on plastic covered mattresses. Most of their experiences were devoid of both love and pleasure. This was definitely not for me. I was going to wait for my knight in shining armor.

I was not kissed until I was sixteen, an age when most of my friends had already "done it," and two or three girls in my class had given birth. I think I did manage to see a penis in high school, I'm not sure. I did have one boyfriend for about six months, and I must have provided manual stimulation, but I do not think I ever actually saw his penis.

The time finally came to go away to college. It was a shock. Not only did I encounter the prevailing sexual attitude, "get all you can," but the racial attitudes were foreign to me. I remember reading the graffiti on the library walls and being outraged. I could imagine uneducated people being dogmatic, but an educated racist seemed an oxymoron.

One weekend evening late in the fall semester I went out with my friend Bill. Most everyone had deserted the campus for the weekend. The bars were empty so we returned home early and decided to hang out in his room. Some of his friends came over, among them a gorgeous guy named Doug whom I had seen around campus but never really talked with. I confided in Bill that I was completely infatuated with Doug! He was "HOT!"

I spent a memorable time talking and drinking beer with the guys. To my delight, Doug devoted the entire evening to me. He was impressed I was down to earth and athletic, unlike many of the other women at college.

Halfway through the evening, I left the room to rinse my eyes because my contacts were uncomfortably dry. It was at this time, unbeknownst to me, Bill planted the seed. He told Doug how "hot" I thought he was. When I returned, Doug asked if I would run with him the next day, and if he could walk me home. "Absolutely," I replied to both.

I was thrilled to be getting so much attention, but was a bit nervous as well. Running and talking were fine as long as it was shop talk. I could handle that, but male-female relations were a different matter. We arrived at my room, and I practically shut the door in Doug's face. I was so unsettled about being with a guy all alone in my room. My God, I mean, my bed was right there! I calmly told Doug I would see him tomorrow. Quickly, he asked me to go to the football game the next day before our run. I said I would see him there. "Good-night."

Doug and I talked through the entire game. I don't remember what was said, but my heart went out to this beautiful person who seemed to have so much hurt inside. So I kissed him gently on the cheek. This shocked us both. So we both ignored the kiss and went right on talking.

Later, when it grew dark, we walked down a wooded road behind campus. He was taking me to get some Haagen-Dazs ice cream because I had argued that Ben & Jerry's was the best. He contended that growing up in Maine had left me devoid of taste and unable to appreciate the finer things in life such as Haagen-Dazs. Half way down the road, he reached for my hand and I panicked. My God! This is the perfect scene for date rape. What was I thinking? I hardly knew this guy! My God, I'm so stupid! He sensed my nervousness as I dropped his hand and did not push the issue. It was at that point I realized how naive and young I really was.

After buying butter pecan Haagen-Dazses, we went to a beautiful pond on campus. Then we walked for hours and simply talked. I decided not only was this guy beautiful on the outside, but, more importantly, on the inside too. We clicked immediately, sharing similar interests. He told me he only wanted to date me and no one else. He told me I was the most beautiful and kindest woman he had ever met and that I was perfect for him. Of course I did not fall for these well crafted lines. Because I understood how naive I was, I put up a huge barricade. My reasoning was that if he was serious he would wait. And wait he did.

The next day, we went running, and I actually ran circles around him. I was in great shape from field hockey and wanted to prove to him I was to be taken seriously. After our run, while we were stretching, he kissed me. It was a simple and innocent kiss placed delicately on my lips. From that run, our first date, our relationship developed very slowly. We became the best of friends. He told me later that I was such a challenge to him, that he never knew I was ever the slightest bit nervous, although he was positive I knew how nervous he was. It was absolutely perfect.

One night Doug was very upset. Since we told each other everything, we talked about the incident that had upset him. That day he had bought me a rose and chocolate cake for no special reason. He always did little things like that to show he was thinking of me. As he was walking to my dorm to deliver the presents, two women friends of his began to follow him. As they were talking to each other, he heard, "He must be bringing those flowers to that white girl of his. I can't understand why he wastes his time with her when there are so many beautiful black women." The other replied: "Maybe he loves her." "Are you kidding, he can't love her, she's white."

Because Doug had grown up in a lily white community and attended exclusive white prep schools, it was important to him to become involved with the black community at college. He now wondered if I was a deterrent to that involvement. I said of course not. I'd love to go to all the Afro-Latin society events. It was then he told me he had not told his parents I was white. His father had told him white women were ugly. His mother, he said, would not even speak to me. Then he turned to me very earnestly and said in a sad, gentle voice, "It would be perfect if you were black." I was furious. If I had said that to him, I countered, he would break up with me in a second. He agreed and said he was very sorry. It was only that he wanted to explain to me that it was going to be difficult.

From that time forward, race became more and more of an issue, not with me or even my family, but with Doug and his family and friends. When his mother found out I was white, she was very disappointed. The black women's community at the college shunned Doug and labeled him as too stuck up to be seen with a black girl. He was an "oreo," all white on the inside. His white football friends told him they were not happy. One bigot stated very firmly that he had "no right to be with a white girl." His black male friends wanted to know if I was different in bed. Most of them wanted to sleep with a white girl just to see what it was like.

Needless to say, I was quite upset. I really did not understand what the big deal was, having been taught that people are people. We all have similarities and differences. Our skin tone should not separate us. Everything came to a head one night when Doug and I were fooling around. We were not making love because neither of us wanted to make that commitment until we were positive our relationship was going to be a lasting one. He told me he put me up on a pedestal above himself and black women because I was white. Again I was very angry. He explained the fascination some black men have with white women and the hatred some black women feel towards white women who date black men. "It is all connected to the slave days when white women were the forbidden fruit." Now, white women are not off limits to the black man. Doug then gave me "Going to Meet the Man" by James Baldwin, a short story which graphically describes the white man's sexual fear of the black man and a young boy's initiation into sexual manhood by watching the hanging of a black man. The boy even becomes aroused watching the castration of the black man just before he dies. Doug and I analyzed this story together. I was amazed and sickened by the whole subject.

Christmas break came and Doug went to Maine with me for a week. He asked what I wanted for Christmas, gold, diamonds or expensive perfume. I simply replied that anyone can give those gifts. I wanted something unique that expressed all his love for me. Nothing expensive and replicable. I had thought the words went in one ear and out the other, but on Christmas he presented me with a doll he had made by hand and sewn himself including the clothes. It was the sweetest thing anyone had ever done for me. I was so touched. I knew at that moment this big, handsome football player was all mine, forever. It was then and there on my bed we lay naked together for the very first time. It was wonderful. It was not actually intercourse, just the beginning phases.

We returned to school closer than ever, determined not to let anyone come between us. Later that month, we began to make love. It all happened so gradually and gently, like being immersed in a warm bath. I really don't recall the specific details. All I know is that it was one of the happiest moments of my life. I was in complete and utter bliss. Life could not be better. We were like brother and sister, only closer. He was so romantic and thoughtful, always planning champagne nights with candle light, just the two of us, or cooking a wonderful dinner to be eaten with soft music and dim lights. I was absolutely in love, one hundred and ten percent. I did not feel guilty we were making love because we both knew this was it. This was forever.

Then spring break came. I was to go home with Doug, but the night before, his mother decided she really did not want me there for more than a day. She called me "a witch," who had "placed a spell on her son." She said I must be a true witch to make her son be this crazy over a white girl. Since Doug and I were determined to spend the break together, she went away for the week and I visited with Doug and his father. We had a wonderful break, and I had an interview at the local TV station for a summer job because I was planning to be near him. His dad and I hit it off wonderfully, and he even wrote me a few times at school.

Some time after spring break, things began to fall apart little by little. Things grew progressively worse until finally one day I said forget it. Doug agreed. We went through a very painful breakup which took place over a two-week period. We cried and hugged and kissed a great deal. It would have continued to disintegrate slowly, alternately clinging and then pushing away. But one night he spent the whole night at another woman's house. I was sick. How could he sleep with someone else? We had planned on us forever.

In the remaining weeks of school, Doug managed to sleep with many women. I was terribly hurt and confused. I had been a virgin and Doug had been with only one girl before me which he "regretted." They were not in love, we were. After college ended that first year, I carried my pain along with the hope that true love would reunite us. While he slept with almost thirty women, I did not even date and shunned men who showed interest. I was waiting for Doug. I was waiting because I was incapable of doing anything else. I had to spend my life with him because I had given him something I could never give anyone else. I had given him a part of myself.

Time moved on and the wounds began to heal. Doug contacted me over the summer a few times and when we returned to school that autumn, we gradually began to spend time together again. Every other week or so he would call me or I would call him and we would tentatively ask the other out for ice cream or a morning run. Our lives were still intertwined and there were numerous occasions when a crisis would occur and we found ourselves turning to each other for support. He frequently expressed interest in getting back together, but because of my pride and despite my conviction that we would be together some day, I shunned his advances, believing the time was not right. He still loved me and I was positive I could love no one but him, but how could I trust him like I once had?

We became best friends again. Junior year, we began joining each other every day for our morning run. Often he cooked me meals and we found we were spending almost all our free time together. By the beginning of senior year, we began to go on platonic dates. God, I loved him so much. I just didn't want to be hurt again, so I ignored his advances and told him we were friends and that was all it would ever be. I tried desperately to suppress my feelings.

Eventually my emotions won and we began dating again. I'll never forget our first, second kiss. He cried and squeezed me so tight. Again, everything was perfect. Then we made love for the first, second time but it was mechanical and cold. I was disgusted. Just a few days before, he had been brimming with emotion. What had happened? When we finished, instead of cuddling, he got up and announced he had to leave. I cried out, "Why are you doing this? What is wrong?" He turned and looked at me and said, "Oh, come on Nancy, you know that sex is just sex to me."

I died right there. A person I had trusted with my life for four years even through bad times, as lover and best friend, had just hurt me more than I ever knew possible.

The remainder of senior year, I refused to speak to Doug, and, although I saw him on numerous occasions, we never spoke again. I made a point of having a fun final semester. I dated other people for the first time. Although it hurt, I was finally free of Doug. I was free of my notion that first love lasts forever. I was free of my responsibility to marry the first man I made love to. If Doug and I had never made love, the relationship would not have had such an impact. I think it took the final time we made love for me to realize that for many people sex is just a physical action and does not imply a deep connection or responsibility to another person. But in my mind, sex will never be just sex. Making love with someone is the most intimate act, and I can only share myself with someone I trust, love and intend to be with for the rest of my life.

8

The Myth

by Shelley Lapree

I approached Steve's doorstep, barely able to see in the pitch black night, my heart beating in my ears. Common sense was telling me to turn back, walk up the hill and across campus to the safety of the bunk in my freshman dorm, where my two roommates who had encouraged me to follow this course of action were peacefully asleep. "Follow your heart," they'd said. My two virgin roommates!

* * *

I'm not sure of the exact time when I became aware of the myth surrounding losing one's virginity. I can't even point to an age range. I only know that at some point in my childhood and pre-adolescence, I became imbued with certain expectations of what it would be like to lose my virginity, to whom I would/should lose it, and what I would feel like when it was over.

Perhaps my mother had told me, or my Girl Scout troop leader, or (more likely) a friend telling me what her mother had told her: "Honey, one day you'll lose your virginity, and it will be one of the most special days of your life. So take your time. Save it for somebody special because it only comes once in a lifetime, and you'll never forget that man." Enforcement of heterosexuality aside, "save it for someone special" seemed as good a credo as any. So I waited and waited and waited. I said "no" many times, waiting and waiting for that special man to come along, "the one," that Prince Charming to whom I'd lose my virginity and with whom, implicitly, I'd fall in love.

* * *

I kept walking toward "his" house even though it didn't feel right. It was easier than stopping, paralyzed with indecision. I knocked on the door because it was better than standing on his porch at 2:00 am feeling like an idiot. His windows were black. Like most normal people, he was probably asleep. This was not going according to plan. In fact, it was verging on the very uncool. It had not occurred to my roommates and me that "Prince Charming" would need to be awakened in order to share the magical moment.

I hoped he hadn't heard my tentative knock resound in the night stillness. "Who the hell is it?" blurted a gruff, sleepy voice from inside. "It's Shelley," I blurted back, realizing instantly that ANY other name would have been a better choice. It wasn't merely the absurdity of the scene which made me want to disappear—young woman tries to seduce man she barely knows by waking him out of a deep sleep. It was even more the picture of the confused and irritated look he must have had when he heard, "It's Shelley" from the other side of his door. Because "Shelley" was not his girlfriend, nor had "Shelley" ever been to his house, nor had any intimacy occurred between them except a good deal of flirting and some kissing, most of which had taken place while he was in a drunken stupor. "Shelley" was a cute 18 year old freshman, in contrast to his worldly 26.

What the hell was "Shelley" doing at his door at 2:00 am, he must have thought. Lacking subtlety as one does when jolted awake, that thought is exactly what came out of his mouth: "What the hell are you doing here?" The possibility of this reaction had not occurred to my roommates and me. Anyone who would answer my advances with "what the hell are you doing here" was obviously not The One. This was not at all what "the myth" had promised my special night would be. I decided right then and there that I would not lose my virginity to Steve.

However, I was in a "spot," and felt I couldn't just walk away. So I asked to come in. I tried to act calm and self-possessed as though, anticipating his not-very-warm reception, I was prepared to overcome it with sexiness and grace. Of course, I had precious little of either, so sat awkwardly on the bed when he offered it. I'm sure he didn't know what else to do with me at 2:00 am, and guessed the bed was what I'd come for. And it was, wasn't it? Or was it? It was kind of fuzzy to me at that point. What the hell was I doing there, if not to sleep with him? Isn't this what my roommates and I had planned in our freshman dorm? Wasn't this going to be the big night when I LOST IT?

Well, yes, it was, but it wasn't supposed to be like this. First of all, he was supposed to be waiting up, restless, unable to sleep because of his burning love for me. My knock on his door was supposed to be like the answer to his silent prayer, as if I'd read his mind from across campus. We were supposed to have a drop-dead kiss in the doorway that would lead to a night of unbridled, loving sex. Oh, and one more thing: he was supposed to be touched and thrilled about my losing my virginity that night. It was supposed to add significant romance and sexiness to the whole affair.

"So what *are* you doing here, Shelley?" he asked. I now knew that whatever else I was thinking, I was going to have sex with this man. One does not walk out into a cold November night, knock on the door of a dark house, wake up a man one barely knows, to what—talk? Chat? Make out, then leave? Play chess? No, none of the above. I had to go through with it. I was now in it for the long haul, a haul which seemed a lot longer and graver than the romantic rendezvous planned earlier that evening.

* * * * *

My roommates and I had sat talking into the night. I was entirely consumed by my crush on Steve.

"So, if you like him so much, why don't you just tell him how you feel." It was about midnight and this conversation had already been going for at least two hours.

"I can't do that!" I retorted. "He'd laugh in my face."

"No he wouldn't," my other roommate, Jennie, offered. "He probably feels the same way you do. I mean, he's the one that's been making all the advances, right? He's been paying all this attention to you, he's obviously really into you, and he practically attacked you at the game today. He just doesn't know how to tell you."

"You think so?" I asked, a glimmer of hope entering my mind. "Well, anyway, it doesn't matter because I'm not doing anything. I'm just going to sit here and go crazy 'til the men in the white suits come to take me away."

My roommates' expressions were kind and sympathetic. I was obsessed with Steve, and there was nothing I could do to change that. I'd never felt this way about a man before. Not that Steve and I shared intimacy or love; we didn't. Rather, we connected socially and intellectually in a way I'd never experienced. I'd never dated someone I admired so much. We'd been dating for three months, and all I knew was that I wanted to be with him every waking moment.

Finally I couldn't stand it any longer. "That does it. I'm going down there right now and tell him how I feel."

"You are?!? Well, all right!!" Jane and Jennie chimed, not sure it was the best idea, but convinced it was better than watching me mope 'til dawn. It sounded so romantic, a passionate confession in the middle of a cold winter night. So we cranked the music, and probably did some field hockey cheers to get the adrenaline pumping even more rapidly than it already was. Then Jane got my diaphragm out of the sock drawer (definitely given to me by my mother, though I have no recollection of that) and said "Here, you better take this."

"I'm not going to SLEEP WITH HIM!" I shrieked. Jane and Jennie crossed their arms and looked at me incredulously.

"Am I?" We all laughed, and probably did some more field hockey cheers to psyche me up for the big night. Then we three bounded out into the winter air. They gave me a rousing send-off as I skipped down "Memorial Hill" to my doom, my virgin roommates standing at the top waving, their choruses of "Follow your heart" ringing in my ears. Memorial Hill. In memory of my virginity.

* * * * *

I sat on the bed. He suggested I take off my clothes and get in. It was most certainly the only thing to do. The nakedness felt extremely odd, and it was very awkward to know him so little on this intimate a level. All of our social compatibility and my admiration didn't seem to count for much when we were in bed. His touch seemed cold and impersonal. We had intercourse, the act as unfeeling and joyless as the word "intercourse" sounds. The pain was so excruciating that I could not hide it, try as I did. "Does it hurt?" he asked. I looked down at the concerned expression on his face and realized that this was a trial for him as well. Inflicting pain on me was simply not enjoyable. He was not in **Nine and One-half Weeks**esque ecstasy, not consumed with passion like they are in the soaps. He was simply enduring it. My idol was having to endure what was supposed to be the most magical moment between two people! I was mortified.

The "most special night of my life" had turned into a nightmare. What had I done wrong? I was supposed to "save it for someone special," and I thought I had. I'd waited and waited and waited. I'd said "no" many times, and been careful to avoid most compromising situations. Steve was the first man I'd ever met about whom I felt strongly. I really admired and respected him, but like many adolescent women, I had mistaken admiration for love.

One hole in the myth surrounding losing one's virginity is the definition, or lack thereof, of the word "special." During adolescence, many young men are "special" to a young woman: the captain of the soccer team, the first boy you kiss, the most popular guy in school. In college as well, many men appear "special": the first man that takes you seriously intellectually; the first man with whom you fool around who you actually aren't embarrassed to talk to the next day; your Teacher's Assistant or Resident Advisor. All of these men fit the definition of "someone special," yet they are not necessarily good people to lose your virginity to. Why? Because the chances are good that you are not in love with them, but rather idolize them in one sense or another. In idolizing or admiring them, you probably don't trust them. In a word, you are probably not really friends.

This was certainly the case with Steve and me. When we were in bed, my vulnerability and embarrassment index was at a lifetime high. As a result, I sincerely wished I was with someone I trusted, someone who was first and foremost my friend. "Someone special" really meant "someone you could trust." There's a big difference. Losing your virginity can be painful and not particularly enjoyable for a woman. As such, it cannot be considered "good sex." Nothing is more trying or intimidating than sharing bad sex with someone. Intimacy, trust, and caring are needed to overcome that vulnerability and embarrassment, to turn it into a positive, romantic experience.

Following that night, Steve distanced himself from me, or rather, he showed no change. I had expected the relationship to advance after sleeping together. It didn't. In effect, I had expected us to fall in love. We didn't. The fact that we'd slept together meant little to Steve, and had little impact on our relationship. Things simply continued in the same noncommittal, flippant fashion until Steve graduated that January.

I remember being quite surprised at the time that sleeping with someone did not necessarily lead to love. This naivete was soon lost, however. The more people I slept with, the more I disassociated sex and love. I had several boy friends that year, none of whom I loved but all of whom I slept with. The sex was not really enjoyable; it was more like a fitness workout. Perhaps the negative experience of losing my virginity lowered my expectations for sex and the sexual relationships that ensued.

Hence the occasion of losing my virginity was hardly the most magical night of my life, nor was it even a special thing to share with a man because we were not in love. It was simply the first time I had sex, followed by many more times just like it but less painful.

Of far greater impact and importance was the first time I "made love," the first time I really enjoyed sex with a man I loved. I consider that to be the real loss of my virginity and my entrance into sexual maturity. Our society ritualizes the physical "popping of the cherry," yet pays virtually no attention to the first time a woman experiences orgasm or the joy of making love. We focus on the act itself, rather than the quality of the experience. This is yet another manifestation of patriarchy in our culture. When a man loses his virginity, explicitly he experiences orgasm. For a woman, however, the two do not necessarily go hand in hand. Our society's emphasis on simply "losing it," rather than on the quality of the experience, stems from this disregard of women's sexuality.

* * *

So why had I waited so long for Steve, who didn't end up being very "special" anyway? After all, in this day and age, eighteen is relatively old to lose one's virginity. Surely there had been other offers?

There had. And for various reasons, some noble and sensible, some just lucky, I had declined. Despite all my criticism of the myth of "saving it for someone special," it served one very positive purpose: it gave me high standards. It made me think very hard when someone suggested we sleep together. It also made me always hold out for something better. I had been sorely tempted to say "yes" several times, but somehow ended up saying "no" even then because I knew those men were not "the one."

My first offer for sex came through the back door, quite literally. He walked through our back door with a crowd of my older brother's and sister's friends one summer night. My older brother, Bob, and my older sister, Nancy, were having a party as they did almost every summer night. Bob and Nancy were 19 and 21, respectively.

Nick, the main character of this story, was the older brother of one of Bob's friends. That would make him about 26. I had just turned sixteen, sixteen going on 21. More than anything, I wanted to be older, attractive to Nancy's and Bob's friends, and to be accepted as their peer rather than their kid sister.

When Nick persisted in paying an inordinate amount of attention to me throughout the party, this seemed to be the answer to my prayers. He would corner me and make passes. When he asked me to go for a walk,

I hesitated. His motives were entirely transparent, though I didn't know how far he wanted to go. Predictably, the teen fear of making a scene won out, and the "cooler," more mature response seemed to be to agree. Nancy cinched the deal by pulling me aside and asking if everything was all right. I imperiously told her I could take care of myself, and whisked Nick out the door.

Our walk led to the barn, and Nick guided me to the sawdust pile, where he took off my shirt and muffled "Let's do it, come on, let's do it" into my neck. The "no" came out of my mouth like a knee-jerk reaction. I didn't know why, I only knew it was the only answer. Suddenly we heard the animated voices of Nancy and Bob approaching. I knew what they were up to; I knew their strategy. They had come to save me from Nick, and frankly I was flattered they cared. Nick pulled me into a horse stall before I could think. There I was hiding from "the enemy"—my brother and sister who were there to protect me—with my "friend," this drunken, lascivious man who was trying to sleep with his brother's friend's pre-pubescent younger sister in the barn. The absurdity of the situation would have catapulted me into hysterics had Nick's hand not suddenly found its way into my pants.

Paralyzed, I let him continue. As my siblings' antics echoed through the barn, he touched me, and lo, it felt good! It really felt good, and the word in my head was no longer "no," it was "yes, yes, yes." I wanted to go through with it and probably would have, had my siblings not given up and left the barn at that moment. I listened yearningly to their familiar, friendly voices trail way toward the warm, well-lit house and found myself alone in the dark, silent barn with an old, pathetic, drunken stranger. The change of scene changed by mind. I walked out of the stall, right out of the barn and didn't stop 'til I reached the safe din of the party, leaving a trail of sawdust in my wake.

What had enabled me to say "no" when I wanted to say "yes?" What inherent mechanism gave me this mature judgment when my sixteen-year-old hormones were lobbying for quite a different reply? I don't have an answer. I can only say that the myth surrounding losing one's virginity—that it would be the most special night of my life—made me hold out for something better, knowing even then that the "most special night of my life" had to be better than a drunken stranger in a sawdust pile.

I refused an offer the following year for the same reason. It was 4:00 am and I was in a Washington, D.C. hotel room in bed with a friend of a friend I was crazy about. I wanted to go through with it so badly, but something told me that "the most special night of my life" was not going to take place in a D.C. hotel room with a man I'd met the day before. The myth was working.

All the credit for my good judgment in these instances does not go to "the myth's" high standards. Some of it goes to my family. Bob and Nancy served as models of what I consider to be responsible sexual behavior. They played myriad roles serving as catalyst, instigator, and presenter of opportunity simply by providing exposure to older people. Simultaneously, they were protector, teacher, counselor and role model. Often they were better positioned than my parents because of their proximity in age. My siblings had a window into my personal life. They knew the cast of characters surrounding me. We overlapped in high school and saw each other at parties. They surely could relate to my growing pains having recently experienced them too.

More than anything, my good judgment is a credit to my parents, whose liberal views on sex and alcohol produced children who exhibited very responsible behavior in these areas. They believed that adolescents were going to drink and have sex whether or not it was permitted. Far better to allow parties in the house with Mom and Dad upstairs than to find us all passed out in a field somewhere. In the same vein, they did not ban sex in the house. When my brother brought his serious college girlfriend home, my mother gave him the option of sharing a bedroom. He declined at the time, but the message to us all was clear: sex, like alcohol, did not have a permanent "No Trespassing" sign attached. For me, as for most of my friends, any "No Trespassing" sign served as a neon welcome mat for violation. The lack of "No Trespassing" on sex took the rush out of things. I did not feel challenged to "break that rule" and run out and sleep with somebody. My parents had shown me that sex was a mature subject, a fact of life, a normal state of affairs, not some lewd, forbidden, titillating act, a rule waiting to be broken.

* * *

When I arrived back at my freshman dorm the morning after I had lost it to Steve, my roommates were still asleep. It was about 6:00 am and the sun was just rising. It looked like it was going to be another crystal clear, cold November day. I stood out in the quad looking over the misty scene and felt empty and disappointed. I had blown it. I could never lose my virginity again, and instead of saving it for "the one," I had given it away to someone who didn't care about me. I blamed myself, and assumed that most women had been able to achieve that perfect night of bliss.

I also felt surprisingly changed. Regardless of how negative and painful the previous night had been, I had lost my virginity and that seemed to count for something. I felt as though I was regarding the world with a newly matured, experienced eye. It seemed as though the world was holding me in slightly higher regard, as an experienced woman, not just a young girl. I felt that somehow I looked different, that it must be apparent on my face. I knew my roommates would want to know everything that happened, and I knew I would guard my newfound secrets. I simultaneously bemoaned the irreversibility of my lost virginity, and reveled in my newfound sense of maturity.

The pretense of maturity and change only lasted a few hours. By noon it had worn off. All that build-up had been a farce. I felt no closer to being an experienced woman than I had the previous day. Everything was the same—except that I had had sex for the first time.

In hindsight, I think our society unrealistically builds up girls' expectations for losing it, setting young women up for disappointment by creating a nearly impossible standard. The myth of losing one's virginity to Prince Charming is a vestige of a time when women married the first man they slept with, or rather, lost their virginity to their husbands. Under those social codes, women were smart to "save it for somebody special." Their marriageability, and consequently their entire social status, lay in their ability to prove on the wedding night that they were virgins, unsoiled and pure.

Times have changed, yet we cling to these traditions, vestiges of social values long since past. Our society needs to attribute less importance to the single act of losing it, and pay more attention to the overall quality of sexual experience in a young person's life. It's still smart to "save it for someone special," but not because virginity is the one thing women "own" or control; not because it represents some sort of power over men and so shouldn't be given away lightly; not because he will necessarily be Prince Charming; and not because you will somehow be inextricably linked to whichever man you lost it to. It's smart to hold out for someone special because you are most vulnerable when having sex for the first time, and it takes a special, caring relationship to make it a positive sexual and emotional experience.

9

Yearning for That Big Moment

by John Mason

As a child I was precocious in many ways. I read early and often, I listened carefully to the conversations of adults and, much to their amusement, was able to parrot their language and ideas with charm and wit. When it came to sex, I was precocious in that my first sexual urge occurred when I was seven. My mother was, in those days, what is known in the East as a "horse woman," meaning that I was dragged from horse show to horse show fully expected to serve as a miniature stable boy. At one of these shows I had my first crush. She was eighteen and to me, thoroughly enchanting astride her big black horse. Throughout the weekend of the show I became **her** miniature stable boy, tagging along in the barns and fields utterly enraptured by her smile and flattered by her proclamations that I was "so cute."

But besides her nice smile, I remember one afternoon the movement of her breasts under her white riding shirt produced within me an odd sensation. It was a bit like feeling hungry except it wasn't in my stomach but somewhere deeper within—an inarticulate urge, a yearning to touch her. I did not know at the time what to think about feeling this way except that it felt good and so for the rest of the weekend her breasts superseded all the rest of her fine qualities which had fascinated me.

Over the next few years my first encounter with the sexual urge took definition from the inarticulatable to the concrete. I associated with older cousins who took great pleasure in "educating" me with vivid, grandiose accounts of their copulations effected in tents, swimming pools, cars, and barns. There were occasions when certain voluptuous female cousins thought it amusing to skinny dip in my presence. I was fascinated by their anatomy and made the connection that my small erection and that roiling, lustful feeling within me was related to the parade of nudity strutting before my eyes. My facility for reading coupled with my appreciation of the female nude led me to pornography and sexual self-help manuals both of which precipitated my first attempts at masturbation—clumsy and horrifying but then not so bad and then kind of fun and finally a lot of fun. . . .

By the time I was sixteen I had had it with speculation about intercourse and unfulfilling gropings with reticent girls. My scientific analysis of female anatomy, sexual positioning, do's and don'ts, and erotic exegeses on the beauty and unique pleasure of an orgasm inside a woman made me yearn for that big moment. The only good thing about not feeling it then was the surety that the moment would inevitably occur.

Snow

One winter day when I was still sixteen and still a virgin, I went on a school sponsored ski trip. We were packed into a touring bus and I sat in the back glancing surreptitiously at an attractive girl sitting next to me. I remember her fragrant hair and soft voice. I remember the mixture of pleasure and anxiety I felt as my penis filled with blood—would she notice?

By the lodge she went one way and I the other (would this story have been different if I had followed her?). At the top of the mountain I pointed my skis downhill and started my run. The first turn to the right was clean and sharp. The second turn to the left was just starting when the tips of the skis encountered an icy rut and crossed. Suddenly I was airborne, the weight of my body somersaulting down the slope. There was flying snow, the sound of metal on metal, the taste of the snow, the sensation of my head striking ice, and a flash of darkness. I lay stunned feeling only the snow and ice in my nostrils and on my face. I looked at my arms stretched out in front of my face and commanded them with my brain to move. When they refused I realized that the only part of me which felt wet and cold was my face. The rest of my body was somewhere else, detached, numb. I knew then that I had broken my neck.

Irony

The moment I became paralyzed was ten years ago. Today I use a wheelchair and will continue to do so for the rest of my life. I can't move my legs or fingers, but my arms function enough so that I can propel myself around. Though I can feel the pressure of someone's touch, I cannot feel normally from the chest down. This means that the affected areas do not register any kind of sensitivity whether a needle's jab or a caress. Indeed when I touch my leg, it feels as if I am touching someone else's.

At its basic level, sex is a tactile function. Its physical success depends on the friction generated between opposing surfaces of flesh. Its physical pleasure depends on very sensitive nerve endings being stimulated in various ways. For a male, the whole body can be sensitive to fingers caressing, a tongue licking and searching, or the light touch of hair brushing across the skin. But as I learned before I was hurt, the ineffable pleasure of skin stimulation was most pronounced when my penis was stimulated. As a result of paralysis, my penis was numb to any kind of touch. Thus my years of yearning for that wonderful feeling of warmth, friction, and moistness surrounding my organ—the thrusting, the pressure, the build up and the climax—would never be fulfilled.

It is a bitter instance of irony that I can still get an erection and have intercourse but feel absolutely nothing physically—one of the great experiences of human existence which I so keenly wanted to enjoy can still be performed but instead of physical pleasure I feel a horrible sensory void.

Mary

In the aftermath of losing my virginity, my ironic situation remains the same, which is disheartening. But my first intimate situation was a positive experience for certain reasons.

Most significantly, Mary made me understand that my paralysis did not prevent her from feeling sexually attracted to me. When we met I was nineteen, paralyzed for three years and very worried that I would never even get the chance to find out what sex could be like in my condition because I assumed that society would view me as an impotent, negligible sexual entity. I knew that I was physically attractive and interesting to be with but would I be able to arouse someone's sexual interest? After our first exchanges of kisses I sensed immediately that as a sexual unit, our desires were in concert. This realization was liberating and exhilarating.

Once we were in bed looking at and touching each other's naked bodies, I learned that the parts of my body that were undamaged were very sensitive to touching and kissing. I learned that I could channel my desire away from what I wanted to feel in my crotch to what I felt around my head and then to my brain. By recalling how it felt to touch my penis with what I felt as she kissed my ear, I was able to generate a high level of sexual excitement which, instead of originating from my genitals, came from my mind. I also discovered that giving Mary pleasure further enhanced the experience. Not only did I have the satisfaction that I could make her feel good, but that the quality of the exchange was not based solely on my climaxing inside a woman. It was instead the achieving of a sense of intimate interaction where all the barriers between us had been shattered and I felt, as she achieved orgasm, that our souls had intertwined.

These powerful emotions happened with Mary because we cared for each other. Even though I was not able to have an orgasm, our first experience together was very positive. I could imagine what people mean when they speak of meaningful versus empty sex, for even though I couldn't physically feel what I had always wanted to, the mental connection and ability to give pleasure made me feel whole as we embraced in our bed.

But Still . . .

The things I learned after my first experience with Mary were reinforced by subsequent experiences with her and other women since. But still, in spite of my knowledge which lets me know I can still attract women, which lets me know that I can make a woman have an orgasm, and which has made me aware of the power and beauty of intimacy, my inability to feel and physically climax is frustrating and saddening. It is strange to be able to generate so much sexual energy from the brain but not to have that visceral and even primal release of energy through orgasm. I have no choice but to recognize that this loss is permanent and mourn that fact unapologetically. I also have no choice but to appreciate the emotional power of a satisfying sexual and spiritual relationship and seek it with courage and optimism.

10

STDs and AIDS

*by Peggy Clarke, Executive Director
American Social Health Association*

Examples abound of men and women catching a sexually transmitted disease from just one act of intercourse—and that certainly includes young people, even young people having sexual intercourse for the first time.

Whether the infection is passed through bodily fluids or by touching infected skin, STDs are fairly easily passed from one person to another. And a lot of people have them: one in five adults, estimates suggest. That's more than 40 million Americans.

Of the 12 million Americans who contract an STD each year, as many as three million of them are teens between the ages of 13 and 19. Sixty-five percent of the new infections occur in persons 25 years or younger.

All this is to say that youth and inexperience do not protect you from an STD. The young and the inexperienced can and do get sexually transmitted diseases—every day.

What are sexually transmitted diseases?

They used to be called venereal diseases or even social diseases; they are sometimes called STDs, but quite simply, sexually transmitted diseases are those bacteria and viruses that can be transmitted through the acts of vaginal, oral and anal sexual intercourse.

Some STDs are transmitted through body fluids like blood or semen; others are transmitted by skin-to-skin contact. Some result in sores, some in bumps, some result in itching and pain, but others can have no symptoms at all. Some are curable; most are treatable; all are preventable. Latex condoms are key.

If left untreated, STDs can result in death, cancer, blindness, heart disease, infertility, sterility and birth defects, among many other complications. If you have any reason to think you might be infected, a visit to your health care provider or the local STD or family planning clinic is in order. Safe, economical, confidential help and treatment are available.

STDs are divided into two categories, bacterial and viral. The bacterial ones are easier, in some ways: Not only treatable, they are, in fact curable. Treatment with antibiotics, and you're done. One problem is that some of them often have few or no discernible symptoms, so many people with these infections aren't aware they have them. This group includes syphilis, gonorrhea, chlamydia and trichomoniasis.

Four million persons contract chlamydia each year. A bacteria easily cured by antibiotics, it is often left untreated because its symptoms—especially in women—often go unnoticed. Frequently women won't know they have chlamydia until it causes complications such as pelvic inflammatory disease or PID, an infection of the female reproductive organs that can cause infertility and ectopic pregnancy.

By the way, chlamydia—like most of the other STDs—can be passed from mother to child during birth. Infants born to mothers with chlamydia may be infected with chlamydial conjunctivitis or pneumonia.

Gonorrhea and syphilis affect far fewer people: 1.6 million between them, but their incidence, especially that of syphilis, is growing: The number of syphilis cases is more than double the number of just 15 years ago—and this is a disease we thought we had all but eradicated.

Unlike bacterial infections which can be cured if detected and treated early, viral STDs are with you for life. Very often chronic infections, they are generally more difficult to treat and have no cure. This group includes herpes, HPV/genital warts, HIV/AIDS and hepatitis.

Herpes affects the largest number of people. We estimate 26 to 31 million people in this country alone have herpes—with as many as half a million new infections every year. Spread by intimate genital or oral contact with the infected area, the virus remains in the body after the initial infection and causes recurrences in about two-thirds of these cases. However, with proper care and treatment, herpes is a very manageable condition.

Perhaps the most quickly spreading STD is genital warts. Caused by the human papillomavirus, genital warts can be visible or invisible, depending on the strain, and have been associated with a number of genital cancers, including cancer of the cervix in women. Twelve million persons have HVP/genital warts, with as many as one million new infections each year. Like the herpes virus, HPV is spread by intimate sexual contact.

While a smaller number of people are infected with HIV/AIDS in this country, the fatal disease's toll is heavy and the numbers are growing at a frightening rate. This rapid increase is in part due to the fact that those infected with one STD—especially those producing sores, even when too small to be seen—may be at increased risk of getting HIV infection during contact with an HIV-infected person. Now, even those STDs previously considered minor can take on fatal consequences. And, of course, the other side of that coin is that HIV infection during contact with an HIV infected person can complicate and increase the dangers of other STD infections. Again, for people who choose to be sexually active, latex condoms are key to preventing the spread of HIV/AIDS and other STDs.

HIV damages the cells in the immune or defense system that fight off infection and disease. As the virus gradually destroys these important cells, the immune system becomes less and less able to protect against illness. Certain life-threatening infections and cancers can then invade the body causing serious illness and eventual death.

The AIDS virus is spread through blood, semen and vaginal secretions of an HIV-infected person. There is no evidence that HIV can be spread through other body fluids such as saliva, urine, tears or sweat. Both men and women can pass HIV to a sex partner through vaginal, oral and anal sex. HIV can also be passed through sharing drug needles. HIV-infected women can pass the virus to their babies during pregnancy or childbirth.

HIV can live in an infected person's body for months or even years before any signs of illness appear. Like the viruses that cause herpes and genital warts, there is no way to get rid of the HIV virus once a person is infected. However, new medicines can slow the damage that HIV causes to the immune system.

Teens often believe that they can tell someone is healthy simply by 'knowing' them and that if someone seems 'nice' they couldn't possible infect them with an STD.

Unfortunately, neither is true.

Teens can and do get STDs. Millions already have them. To ignore reality is to put your present and future health at risk. And the sad part is that prevention and protection are simple, easily available and cost literally pennies.

For people who choose to be sexually active, latex condoms used properly (most brands come with directions) during every single sexual act provide protection against a whole array of STDs, both bacterial and viral, as well as against pregnancy.

Spermicides can provide *some* protection against *some* diseases, as can contraceptive sponges. Birth control pills provide NO protection against STDs. Next to abstinence, latex condoms are your best protection.

Why take the risk? Part of growing up is learning to take responsibility for your behavior, including your sexual behavior. If you have made a thoughtful, mature decision to begin sexual activity, make it a responsible decision as well by protecting yourself.

AIDS and other STDs are no fun.

11

In Search of a Definition

by Jack Watson

I often feel "left out of the loop" in society's discussion of virginity since I am gay. I've found consistently that many of society's definitions weren't shaped with me in mind. They simply do not apply. There are also the misunderstandings that make the situation even more complex. Some people equate homosexuality with promiscuity and there's often a silent assumption that gays and lesbians are always engaging in sexual behaviour, all the time and everywhere.

These different issues don't mean that I don't attempt to find some meaning (or solace) in the definitions. What is a virgin? Can you tell the difference when you see someone downtown or in the car next to you on the freeway? For the longest time, I hoped that wasn't the case. I was afraid somebody would know and laugh at me for being one. Madonna doesn't seem to have much of a problem being "Like a Virgin," but that's not as bad as being one.

I've been embarassed for years about being a virgin, and it's not a topic you bring up at the dinner table or even with a good friend. It's hard to figure out what is right and not force yourself to do something with someone just to be rid of the awful label. Is the label so awful, though? Is it all good, either? I know some people who believe it's terrible not to be a virgin up until marriage and other people who think there is nothing worse.

Faced with these dilemmas, it was difficult to figure out whether I wanted to keep the label or not. It's funny that I can get this far in life and still not be clear on the subject. I've been trying to think up some definition that is of more help to me, figuring out just what virginity means to me. Words and concepts like virginity help all of us better define who we are and who we would like to be. As I will explain, I didn't lose my virginity just for the sake of losing the label. It was quite unexpected.

I am 21 years old and a senior in college and, over the past few years, I have been learning how to live my life to its fullest. I have come out to most of my friends and close relatives and I find that being gay is just another facet of who I am. Some of my high school and college years were filled with turbulence associated with coming out, but finally I'm settling down into a very successful and enjoyable life. My career plans are taking shape and I'm about to graduate. I also just had the experience of (finally) losing what I felt was my virginity.

I am involved with the gay group at my university and I sometimes hear criticism related to the intentions of such a group. Anyone who knows the Bisexual Gay and Lesbian Student Alliance (BiGALSA) realizes that we create programming to lend support to fellow bi, gay and lesbian students and attempt to educate ourselves and the university community about political and social issues that affect us both as students and human beings. Some people argue that our group should not be allowed to exist through the Student Programs office at our Catholic university, alleging that we "encourage homosexual sex."

Much of the support that BiGALSA provides relates to the issue of "a gay identity." This includes a sexual identity which is usually difficult to envision, since the concept of virginity is mysteriously missing. When students come into our office, afraid to talk about being gay or lesbian, we try to help them feel not so excluded from the rest of the world. We strive to appear just as normal as we are and serve individually as role models—people who are smart, funny and trustworthy. Often the discussion turns to romantic relationships and the difficulties and joys they bring. The more one learns about gay and lesbian relationships, the more one realizes that there is essentially no difference from heterosexual relationships. I've found, however, that this virgin question remains longest unanswered.

I get the feeling that heterosexual people, especially younger people, may often feel trapped by the clearly-defined meaning of virginity in our society. It's obviously there, everywhere we turn, whether it be television, movies in the theater, the infamous Harlequin romance section of our local supermarket or just magazines . . . light reading . . . even commercials! We are flooded with images of pretty, blemish-free women walking hand in hand with tan, flawless Mr. Right, his teeth white like sugar. The sexual message in these advertisements is not just subliminal either. Sex sells products—all of the numbers and bottom-line revenue reports are in and the company which targets the audience and sells us what we like can turn quite a profit. And we like virginity.

The images are strong and the message clear. There can be no mistaking it—either you are one or you aren't. It's fair to mention here, too, that virgin has long been considered the more desirable label, although that may be changing. And it's generally understood that you don't ever have to tell anyone on which side of the scale you fall—except maybe a good friend—and only if that friend tells you first. The problem for me is that this applies only to heterosexual relationships. I'm not heterosexual and never thought I was, so am left without a clue what "virgin" means to me.

Necessary to our traditional mental picture are a penis and a vagina. Penetration of said vagina by said penis is what is generally accepted as the act of losing one's virginity. If this is the final definition in its entirety, then I am a virgin and will be one forever. I don't think I'm a virgin, though. True, I have never been present or involved in the above described combination (which, by the way, I accept as a legitimate and beautiful union of man and woman). But is it true that I can't lose **my** virginity when straight people can lose **theirs**?

Amusing ironies abound in the whole gay and lesbian experience. For instance, many people (mostly ignorant) assume that all gays and lesbians are so very sexually promiscuous, yet we can't even lose our virginity! But I want to bring in some serious talk: I know what it's like to lose my virginity—I've lost mine very recently. Surprisingly, it happened mostly in my mind. I didn't know how it would happen and was very scared.

I expected it to be anal intercourse. It wasn't . . . entirely. We tend to keep most people in our lives at an arm's distance. Sometimes we let people get closer or pull them closer when we feel safe and emotionally linked. That can be in the form of a hug or maybe telling a secret you thought you wouldn't tell anybody. In any case, you choose to let someone in—you let down your defenses and say, "This is who I am." You probably wouldn't say that out loud (although you could), but the other person understands immediately that this is what you mean.

I had the good fortune to fall in love with a wonderful man about six months ago. It took a long time to allow myself to open up to him, to tell him I loved him. He's loving and tender. His friends admire him for his many fine qualities. I was afraid that he was too perfect for me or that something would go wrong. I eventually decided, with some encouragement from him, thank God, to be honest about my emotions and my very strong feelings. I decided to give it a try—sort of that "Better to have loved and lost than never to have loved at all" thing. We both decided to love each other unreservedly, regardless of whether or not people approved. We spend as much time together as possible, talking, meeting for lunch, even skipping class, learning more about each other every day. I feel safe, truly loved when he's with me, and when we hold hands walking down the street. I used to think that gay people did that to cause a scene in public or upset people, but I'm thinking only of myself when I hold his hand. It feels good for me, very natural. And it would be stupid not to hold his hand, considering the benefit to us both and the amount of time we walk together. He has become sort of a "soul mate." We decided to ignore the fear that we should hide our love.

There was a distinct moment when I felt I had lost my virginity. One night when we were up late talking and laughing, I felt so good inside. In a wave of warmth, I felt whole . . . as if I would never be alone. In this safety, I didn't want there to be any distance between us and I felt him inside my heart, as if he were sharing it with me. No secrets and no fear. The best way I can describe it is that I felt older and wiser. It felt like I had lost a piece of ignorance that I would never have again.

A woman friend of mine was raped during my first year at college. It was a terrible time for all of us who wanted to make things better for her. Naturally, it took a long time for her to deal with the trauma and understand that she was not to blame. It is hard to know what to say or not to say, how to be supportive when something like this happens to a friend. For some, the terror of being violated by rape is compounded by the issue of virginity. Many people assume that the actual physical act of sexual intercourse causes a loss of virginity. I disagree. I believe that if a person has been raped, he or she can still be a virgin. Rape is an act of violence even in the case of date rape, not an act of love by any stretch of the imagination. Some rapes come from the attacker's insecurity with gender roles. For example, some men are misogynists, that is, they are filled with feelings of anger and hatred toward women. Rape can be caused by an outburst of this anger. Other men feel insecure about their masculinity, they want to prove to their friends that they are "real men." Maybe they are afraid they are gay and want to prove (to themselves) that they are not. Often men who are extremely insecure with their sexuality are afraid of other gay men, that they might rape them in a fit of anger and fear in order to vilify and defile them so that they can hate them more. This is obviously not love. A person's virginity is not involved in a rape.

A good portrayal of this personalization and "claiming" of virginity occurred in the movie, "The Color Purple." Whoopie Goldberg's character, Celie, is talking to Shug, her husband's mistress (whom she gets along with really well), about how she doesn't enjoy sex with her husband. "Most time I just pretend like I ain't even there. He don't know the difference. He don't ever ask me how I feel . . . he never asks me nothin' about myself. He just climb on top of me and do his business.'' Shug says surprised, "Do his business . . . why Miss Celie . . . you sound like he going to the toilet on you." Celie then says, "That's what it feel like." In what I consider the best line in the movie, Shug then says "Why then Miss Celie . . . that mean you still a virgin." Just as confused about virginity as we are, Celie says, "Yeah . . . because don't nobody love me."

As my mom used to say, "When in doubt, use a dictionary." Webster's doesn't help much, but it does provide some entertaining definitions. First among many for "virgin" is, "an unmarried woman devoted to religion." Not exactly a role I can identify with. Another definition is "an unmarried girl or woman." So, virginity applies only to women? I read on. "Free of impurity or stain." I close the book. This is copyrighted 1990. So much for my faith in the dictionary. So I boldly forge ahead to find the definition which works for me.

The more I think about it, the dictionary definitions anger me. I'm sure they perpetuate the same misunderstanding which makes virginity taboo. A word which is closely associated with virgin is "chaste." Chaste is defined as "innocent" and "celibate," pure in thought and act. I know many "pure" people who are no longer virgins. Is Webster talking in an abstract sense then? In my bewildered indignation, I arrive at a novel concept: virginity is a right or possession to be treasured and someday given to share with another person. If you can accept that, then it follows logically that something of this intimate value cannot be taken away from a person. Virginity is yours and only yours—to share, when and if you choose.

So I chose to share my virginity with a very special person. I let him get closer to me—emotionally and physically. I was scared and so was he. That's part of it, too, I think. It is through the resolution of the fear that our bond grows stronger. A trust is developing which gives me an intense strength. I feel invigorated and loved. I am no longer a virgin.

Ever since junior high I was afraid I would lose my virginity in a bad or accidental way. It was such a mystery and nothing I could claim as my own. I guess I figured it was one of those things that was out of my control, like puberty or homework. I didn't have to plan puberty, it just happened, and well, no one can prevent homework. It was just recently that I was able to realize that my virginity is **mine**.

Virginity doesn't belong to a rapist or a jeans commercial. It can't be bought or sold. It's really a wonderful feeling to have this new thing called virginity which I can tuck away into my heart or my mind and bring it out to share with another person when it feels right. It follows that everyone should, by all means, lose their virginity at the appropriate time for each person.

So, here's my attempt at a definition: virginity (n):

> a feeling of fear that causes a person to feel he/she will be alone in life or that emotional and physical union with another person is impossible—only recognizable after lost.

I got the feeling as a kid that people didn't want to talk about how they lost their virginity. My mom will not tell me how she lost hers. My Dad won't either. And I wouldn't ask them. I haven't heard many good stories about one losing one's virginity. They've all been pretty traumatic or something the person would rather forget. I've even heard people say they wished it hadn't happened. I can only assume they haven't truly lost theirs yet.

I feel like the owner of "Bob's New and Used Cars," trying to convince you that this ol' body is just as good as new. "Once used, not amused, good as new!" Sort of a "recycled virginity." This is not what I mean. I do mean, however, that no one else's definition is necessarily going to be right for you. Gay, straight, black, white, purple—every human has the need to lose it. It's one of the things that makes life a beautiful, worthwhile experience. However, just as I am not **bound** by what someone else has determined to be my virginity, neither are you limited by my definition. Put some thought into the way you want it to happen. Then, when the time is right, make it happen.

12

Don't Blow It

by Richard James

Jesus, the promised land! Within a week of the end of my junior year of high school, I had myself convinced I had come into my own. I was prepared to take over. Life was definitely one big movie and I was ready to get the game ball, the motorcycle and the girl and strut off into the sunset.

At the second party of that summer, uncharacteristically, I found myself separated from my best buddy Steve and other football friends and talking to two girls at the same time. Shari was a super-cute Filipino. Golden smile. I must have paid considerably more attention to her because her friend flecked off into infinity and there I was one on one and ready for love. Actually my first inclination was to go to the bathroom or make a phone call or try to find a ride or check the tree in the front yard to make sure it was still there or go and find and cling to my friends. Something, some sort of voice from deep within my consciousness, however, told me, forced me, to stay. Perhaps it was that assuring smile. There didn't seem to be any awkward silences. I actually liked the things I said. I think I might even have been having fun just talking to her. It seemed like for once she was also making some effort, taking half the burden of continuity off my inadequate shoulders. She even seemed to be having fun. She was a pleasing contrast to the lily white ball-cutters I had previously pursued.

The party was getting ready to switch locations and something, probably the same primal voice that had just spoken through her smile, told me to follow and persist. I wish I could have pursued for the sake of the easy conversation but of course one good turn deserves another, and I was definitely achievement-oriented, and my hormones were kicking in full throttle. I must have said, "So, I'll see you over at the other party, right!"

"So, I'll see you at the other party right?" "So, I'll see you . . ." about ten times.

"Jesus, we're only going across town. Relax." She ribbed me and I was actually able to laugh at myself.

"Better yet, why don't you just ride with me." I took that as a profession of enduring love, or at least some promise of something, which I realize now was a very skewed assumption. We rode over to the other party, and I was wrenching my brain for something smooth and catchy and intelligent to say to cause a detour. To my surprise I thought of a thousand things. The only trouble was that I couldn't picture anybody but guys in seventies clothing in afternoon movies saying them. I also would have had to have been twice as drunk, or in my football uniform, at least the spikes.

We went to the party and things became scattered. My friends gave me a hard time and I remained silent. She actually wanted to talk to other people, which my adolescent brain interpreted as a slight. I began to get nervous. I drank. That didn't help at all. It actually seemed to make me more nervous. In fact, drinking never did anything at all for me except make me feel bloated, flushed, and once in a while sick when I came home and tried to sleep.

Anyway, I tried to fight the alcohol and continue my pursuit. I saw her again in the kitchen and what did I do? I immediately asked her if she wanted a beer. I couldn't believe that was the only thing to come to mind. She said 'no' to my disbelief, and to my excitement, for I somehow made the irrational conclusion somewhere in my brain that a girl who had the nerve to say 'no' to a beer had the same to say 'yes' to wonderful sex and wonderful me. I was making insane connections. I also thanked god because another beer would have made me slur and lose my remaining edge. The talk was less fluid now. Dammit, I thought, I have to get back in that van, more specifically, in the back of that van. Yes, in a town regurgitating BMWs and Buicks, she had a van, a shining symbol of difference and rebellion. Jesus, a van!

I was too close, at least in my own mind, and I panicked. I went out and walked in the night air, trying to breathe the alcohol away. I considered just walking home. If I had, of course, she probably would still be in love with me, as a man who can walk away in the face of potential orgasm is so rare in this sex-desperate society. I certainly hadn't learned that yet though. I hadn't learned anything. A voice told me to go back in there and go for it; dammit, you're a senior, you're one of the best athletes in the school; she's a year younger, she's got a van, for god's sake, go.

I went. Everything was breaking up. My friends were leaving. Big moment. Big, big moment. I hedged. I slipped into the bathroom and looked in the mirror. Pre-game talk. I slicked my hair with water as I always did before putting on my football helmet. What the hell did I do *that* for? I grabbed a towel and tried to dry it. What the hell did I do that for? I was a mess. Screw it, I thought, I'm going for it. For what I wasn't sure. I walked out and she was with a bunch of her friends. Dammit. I slinked over, hoping the crowd would disperse and leave us alone, but of course it didn't. They all went right out in one big nebulous glob and started to file into the van. I caught her in front of the radiator grille. I tried idiotically to act as though I just happened to be there. I blurted out a "Hey," trying to be as nonchalant as possible, which was none at all.

"What," she returned, totally devoid of emotion. Good Lord, what happened, my mind pleaded to the heavens.

"Uh, what are you guys up to?" The depths of idiocy to which intelligent people will sink in the face of the big prize still astound me, and perhaps this was the first time this issue was brought to bear in my mind.

"What do you think? We're going home." Dammit. Where before she had poked fun at me, now she was giving no quarter. It didn't seem fair. I tried to stay cool while flailing.

"Whose home?" seemed cool enough.

"Well, Kristen is going to Kristen's house and Jen is going to Jen's house. . . ." Still no reprieve. I felt like slunking off into the shadows and trying to figure out a way to get back to sixth grade. My feet didn't, almost wouldn't, move. This was it, I had stepped into the batter's box and taken two useless swings. I don't know why, but it then also became clear that despite the enjoyable conversation, the easy laughing, the simply pleasurable company, this adversarial nonsense had to transpire; she had to pitch and I swing. Nice as she was, different as she was from the pristine hags, she too knew the hard-to-get routine and seemed to deem it necessary. While I was baffled by its emergence, perhaps I somehow accepted its necessity too, because, as I said, I stood there and swung. To simply step out of the game and say, "Why do we do this? You know I really like you and we're young and I'd really like to kiss you and maybe hug and see what happens then, so let's check it out" didn't appear as an option. I was entirely focussed on infiltrating that van. I did my best not to sound corny.

"Well, do you think Rich could get a ride to Rich's house?" Not bad, I thought, viscera pounding and thumping in the seemingly eternal moment that the proposition hung in the air.

"You don't live anywhere near me." Goddammit, stop this, I thought. She has ten girls in that thing and there's no way they can all be geographically compatible. I didn't think I had anything left.

"Yeah, you're right, I'll hike it." My house was way beyond normal walking distance, probably five or six miles, but I had often run home to try to burn off alcohol, so I considered it a legitimate option. I didn't see any humor in my utterance. Essentially I had given up, cashed in, been pushed to the point of honesty, but I doubt if it was the honesty that kept me alive. I would like to think so. However, now having been through more sophisticated versions of this scenario, I am more apt to attribute my revival to some sort of natural reverse Murphy's type law of sex. The basic tenet of this law is that just, and sometimes only, when one has been driven to wit's end, when the reserves of persistence and hope have seemingly been exhausted, when one's tolerance for gamesmanship and unrequited effort have withered, causing one to doubt whether romance, or at least sex, is worth the infinite time and effort that we ambitiously devote to it, something excellent and exciting and rewarding will happen to keep us convinced, hungry, happy to renew our subscription.

And revived I was, as she started laughing at my humorous dejection and pushed me, saying simply, "Get in." Now of course I was levitated by the new life, relieved at not having to walk, and totally confused. Was she just being nice, and if she was, was I going to look like a complete jerk when I continued my propositioning? But she was nice and warm again, and there was physical contact. She flirted with me, that could not be denied.

My mind raced for something smooth to say as she proceeded to drop off her ten friends. During that process, she didn't say anything and I didn't say anything and her friends ignored my presence. I didn't have to make any effort to appear preoccupied. I wasn't sure if she knew where I lived. We crossed town, coming dangerously close to home. Still, the odd ceremonious pact of silence was upheld.

Suddenly we were heading for my street. Mind racing, I panicked but recovered with aplomb. "I can't go home yet," I blurted.

"What?!" She said with genuine inquisitiveness, squinting her eyes and shaking head. She thinks I'm a weirdo. Hey, at least we have something in common, I think I'm a weirdo too.

"Well, you see, uh my parents, uh, you know, think I'm a little shy so, uh where other kids aren't allowed to stay out too late, I, uh have to, that is, I'm not allowed to come home too early, uh, have to stay out long enough to really exercise my social skills. Uh, what do you think of that?"

I was grasping for a laugh. Jesus, please laugh.

She laughed and continued the conversation, "I think you're weird."

While that is perhaps my favorite thing to hear now, as it implies uniqueness and enigmaticism, and as I believe these are the greatest sources of attraction, it was crushing then. Damn, she's right, I'm weird. Dammit, she's turning down my street, it's over. Dammit. Why am I the one on the stand? Why does the guy always have to keep things flowing? Dammit, what is this? All right, no time for that, last chance. Do it, go for it, you'll never have to talk to her again. It took sixteen years to get alone in this van with this girl and there's no way I'm waiting another sixteen.

"You know where I live?" I found that odd. Good? Bad? I didn't know. I didn't know how to give myself the benefit, for the purpose of sanity preservation, in a world full of doubt.

"Yeah." As she said it, though, she drove right by my house. It didn't even cross my mind that this may have been intentional. I accepted it as serendipity. Again I tried to maintain a veneer of calm while my blood took random express trips through my body and brain.

"Well, do you want to take me home, or. . . ."

"Or what?" she was still playing but just a shade more nicely.

"Uh, well, I don't know."

"You don't know?"

"Well, uh, I mean, I don't know."

"Well, how can I know, if you don't know?"

"You know."

"I do?"

"Yeah, you know."

"Well . . . I don't know."

"Well, you just drove by my house, you know."

"I did? I didn't know."

"You didn't?"

"No."

"Really?"

There was a silence, not quite standoffish, but not quite comfortable. Then, thank the powers that be, we both started laughing. Then another silence. Then I simply offered, "Do you want to go to the beach?" I remember how genuine and soft and innocent it felt to say, to offer as a kind invitation to a new friend. I also remember feeling like a giant hypocrite because I knew my intentions were far from innocent and far from the beach. I knew as the words spilled forth that my scheming was beginning to work. At least I hoped so. Again I wonder what she was thinking about my little suggestions. I also can't help pondering what might have happened if we could have just talked straight; maybe that would be less romantic, I don't know.

Anyway, she complied and my exaltation and concomitant panic allowed no space for lengthy reflection. This had to be acquiescence, right? She is ten meters from my front lawn, but doesn't want to drop me off. This must be a sign of unbridled lust. I don't know if this was a residue of the great race to sex mentality, of suggestive beer commercials, or of plain American optimism, but there must be something skewed in such an assumptive way of thinking. Date rape is a much-discussed issue now; it wasn't then. I don't think I had the potential for such or ever will, but I was surely, at least in hope, equating a walk on the beach with a roll in the van, and that's a hell of a leap.

Then again the beach really held no allure at the moment. I knew to get to the beach we had to pass the most excellent make-out spot in New England, North Lake Drive. Not that I had ever made out there. I had never even driven there.

Where before panic had forced me into spontaneous near-wittiness, now presumption made me into a blunt near-jerk. Or maybe an honest jerk. Not completely honest, though. I just simply asked, "Have you ever been down North Lake Drive?" Of course she had. She must have. Still, she played along. No, she said, she hadn't. Maybe she was being as artificial as I. That possibility never crossed my mind then. I felt like that was my job. Maybe it wasn't our faults; maybe we had just been taught for so long that any kind of direct approach to anything was rude or wrong or just not the norm. She drove down the twisted road slowly and I swallowed repeatedly, trying to assure a steady voice as I finally offered, "Let's pull over" with no attached explanation, excuse or attempt at humor. It was the first honest thing I had said. She just said "okay." Simple, also honest. Not very romantic, but I didn't need any more to make my blood flow. We talked for maybe a minute of nonsense. Even though I must have been assured now, I was nearly twitching. I tried to tighten every muscle in my upper body for a moment and then relax. It worked a little. I thought a million thoughts in that minute. The dominant ones were: did I want to go out with her, I don't know; am I still drunk, I don't know; what time is it, I don't know; what am I doing here, I don't know. Yes I do! I'm coming into my own, coming of age, I'm tasting the fruit. I also knew that I wasn't that into coming into my own, which I had tried only a few times and not enjoyed that much and felt odd about. Still, the fruit was making me nervous. Again I went through the pep talk process. Dammit, go for it. She's definitely interested. What the hell will you say to Steve if you chicken out. (This trial in front of peers, by the way, I have found is the most ridiculous motivation for sex that has ever existed, but I must admit it was in my mind). What the hell will you say to yourself? Does everybody talk to themselves like this? I'm definitely weird. I also think I'm horny. Damn, she's cute. Blah, blah, blah, okay, here we go.

I cut her off in mid-trivia. "Hey," I actually said it with some softness, tenderness.

"Hey, what" she said softly, smiling beautifully. I tried not to stare at her like she was a complete novelty. I almost wanted to jump to "I love you," or at least, "I really like you." Instead, in the height of adolescent boneheadism (Actually it can't be blamed on adolescence, as boneheadism still seems to have a strong foothold in many of the slightly more adult dealings I learn about) I continued to try to be suave, assertive, clever.

I leaned right over into her face and tried not to stumble as I inquired, "What have you been thinking about all night?" In terms of effectiveness, it must have been a pretty decent line, because she just smiled and liplocked me. The point is though, that it was just that, a line. I didn't care what she'd been thinking about unless it was indeed what I hoped. Perhaps it would have been highly comedic if she had actually told me. "I've been thinking about the guy who originally derived the quadratic formula, can't remember his damn name." "I've been thinking about whether or not my mom has a drinking problem." "I've been thinking about how foolish it seems to follow a god who seems to have a problem with an emotion as petty as jealousy." Anything. She continued to play along though and I can't complain. I tried to keep up the suave act. "Hey, what's it like in the back of this thing?"

I wasn't one-tenth as knowing as my words might have suggested. It was maybe only the fifth time I had lain horizontal with a girl. She had a great warm soft mouth. She let me fumble with her bra for about ten seconds, then took the whole shirt, T-shirt and bra off in a swipe of the hand. I was in her arena, clearly, and I was enjoying it, no doubt. The thing was that I still tried to appear knowing. There was nothing wrong with being out of my league. I didn't even have a league. I could have learned so much so quickly, as I knew nothing of sensuality. How many males do? And I did learn, but only despite myself. She kept having to wrestle me into comfortable positions and stop the kissing so that we might start over again in a more pleasing way. I tried to caress, but I'd bet it was probably more like grabbing. She didn't seem to mind helping me and I should have seen that this was beautiful, but instead I continued to try to move like I knew something. She moved my head around gently so I would kiss her neck and shoulders, which of course I hadn't thought of. She was warm and nicely toned. I could have been happy with that for at least ten years.

She also had a very mature sense of progression. She had straddled me from the start. This was a new one on me. She thrusted. I was lost. I very delicately, gingerly approached the magic zones. I was used to closed legs and blocking hands at which I had always receded. Thankfully the game had always stopped there for me. It was absurd and detestable to me to think of fighting my way into a girl's underwear. So I just did my best, which couldn't have been very good, but for all I know might have been as good as anybody else. I couldn't even spell clitoris, let alone find one. Still, she seemed to enjoy it, and I enjoyed her enjoyment.

It was sufficient for her to return the favor ten thousand fold. She was rubbing it all the while and, amazingly, I'm not sure if I even noticed for awhile because I was so intrigued and ambitious. I definitely began to notice. Then to exalt. Oh my god, she's going to touch it!

Well, what can I say but that she did and not subtly or without purpose. While much discussion had been devoted to this mysterious subject, the actual feeling had never been touched upon. She did a far better job of it than I ever could. It was fantasmal to say the least. My brain disengaged. Everything flexed. I was hooked. First touch and fully hooked.

From that night on, my mind began to run away with alarming frequency to sex-land. I had to know what it was like. I called her the next day and tried to talk normally. I wanted her to come right over, but my newly discovered religion and purpose in life was pitted against sixteen years of the old one. I was to leave for football camp on the Sunday after that Magic Friday.

At camp I remained obsessed with the very immediate future of my sex life, only a week away, and my body chemistry was very concerned with the future of my genes. Consequently it kept me up half the night, despite the triple daily practices. This didn't help me impress all comers. I found myself falling asleep in the night sessions, and spending the last half of the third practice yearning for bed.

The worst, of course, was that she was a really nice girl, and open, willing to talk about anything. I didn't. I couldn't. I said I learned to carry on two conversations, but not necessarily two good ones. I could have learned a lot from her, just as a person, but also as a female, and also, she being Filipino, as somebody with a different perspective on our little hamlet. More guilt, for not talking to her with more genuine interest, and for feeling like I was harboring this secret agenda. Not that it wasn't obvious and not that she wasn't concurring. Still, spending time seemed tedious, as did talking, as did anything. I'd want to talk to her but the moment we were together the drive went into eleventh gear. I think the fact that I hadn't ever really beaten off added to the addiction.

When I returned home, the experiences never seemed as exciting as the first, despite the advanced sexuality. The first touch had come with very little expectation, and no time to fantasize. Now I was drilling the episodes into the ground before they even happened. Like anything, we are capable of building up sex so much that it has no choice but to let us down in some way. I tried to talk to trusty, lusty Steve about it. However, with him painting me as some sort of conquering sultan, all that came out was the triumph and ecstasy, not the confusion.

* * *

I had one condom. I don't know why or where I got it. Steve thought I needed more. I had no idea why but didn't ask. Despite our foul-mouthed ranting and chivalry, we had never discussed the actual use of such a device. I acted like I knew what to do. Actually I thought I did. I had come across a little book with a pictureless cover in a back room of our house once. All I could remember from its forbidden pages was a picture of a rubber blown up like a balloon, being held by a man in a sterile looking white suit.

We went to a drug store and lurked around for about a half an hour. I was trying to get Steve to do the dirty work for me, sure that somebody's mother was going to see me at the counter. My face filled with blood and flushed repeatedly. I giggled uncontrollably. I am an ardent supporter of sex. A big fan. It can be a great experience. But if you have a hard time dealing with the experience of buying a simple latex product, you're probably not ready for the big shebang.

Later that evening Shari and I sat around a little table in the deserted house of one of my friends and talked for a while, then played some kind of game, like maybe Trivial Pursuit, for about ten minutes. Then we started to get drunk, at least I did. Me and my infinitesimal tolerance.

Time began to swim by quickly. Too quickly. The next thing I knew my friend was chasing his girl around the house. Now the alcohol was dictating my priorities and feeling like sleeping, I lay on the couch. Shari lay on top of me and rubbed my wang and my priorities immediately changed. Then we were upstairs.

Thankfully, the alcohol wore off a little. We hunted for an appropriate room, found one and shed clothes with alacrity. She started with her amazing crafts and I bluntly stopped her. I'm not sure precisely what I said. I am sure that it wasn't an eloquent expression of the fact that I felt close to her and in some way love for her and that I thought if she felt the same then maybe we should try to express these things in a more deeply intimate physical way. I said something like, "Do you want to do it?" I didn't even ask if she had ever done it before. I knew she had gone out with a much older guy who wore a devo suit and just assumed she had. Oddly, I think I had her fooled into thinking I had too.

Regardless, she wanted to and she told me she wanted to and we did. Sort of. I made the awkward break to dig the latex protector out of my recently shed jeans. This is perhaps the only thing that is the same for me now with regards to sex. Stopping to get a condom is strange and unnatural, but totally essential with the AIDS epidemic.

Okay, I've been depicting myself, for the most part as a bumbling fool with a light veneer of knowingness. Maybe the truth is I was doing all right, pretty average for the bold course I was facing. I wasn't so bad. I was trying. I wasn't completely run of the mill. I was excusable at worst. Until now.

Now I acted like I knew exactly what I was doing when I had absolutely no idea. No clue. How could we guys have talked about sex so much and not covered the mechanics of the situation?

I fumbled for the sheath. Of course it was in the last pocket I searched. Small irrational panic. OK, found it. Couldn't open it. Goddammit. All the while my changed anatomy was springing about, getting in the way, feeling funny when I walked back to the bed. It made me laugh, thank god. Okay it's open. Why is it all rolled up? I had only seen a condom unravelled, and I had immediately thrown away the instructional box that my new ones came in, to make hiding them easier. My mind flashed back to the obscure little book in the obscure little room of our obscure little house with the little man in the sterile white suit. I looked at my member. Wow! I looked at her. WOW! I unravelled the rubber and blew it up like the man in the picture. Great, no holes. I looked over at her. "No holes." She had no response.

All right, now to slip it on and let's see what all the hype is about. What the. . . . How the h. . . . What's the. . . . , why didn't somebody tell me how to do this. Why the hell didn't I ask. What the hell is the story. I pulled, stretched and prodded the thing, and simultaneously my thing, in a frenzied way. I felt a great pressure of time, although I'm sure I had no concept of the idea of losing the moment. After all, I had kept the moment alive for about three weeks. Finally, with no words from her, I bailed out. "It's too dark in here; I can't see what I'm doing. Don't go away."

She said only, "hurry" which maybe should have been comforting or maybe even flattering, but had the effect of adding more pressure. I didn't even think to ask for her help, or maybe her sympathy, or maybe for her to share in the newness of the ordeal. I still can't imagine what her thoughts must have been while I masqueraded and bumbled. Especially when I inflated the thing with my mouth and didn't laugh. I don't know how she refrained from laughing. Perhaps it was more like a freak show than a comedy routine. I felt as though this were all happening on stage, or, worse, on the field. I kept up the facade as well as I possibly could. If I had had a drop of honesty or humility, we probably could have shared the comedy of the moment. Maybe we would have felt in love. Maybe we would have made love.

I was sweating profusely as I bolted to the bathroom. There I tried to get a grip on myself. My organ was starting to become raw and recalcitrant from my trying to force it into my post-inflation unravelled bunched up elastic nemesis. I held it with one hand apologetically. Oh my god, that's why it comes all rolled up like that. No. No way I can sneak out to the car for a new start. Even at this point I was trying to salvage my pride and image with a girl who would have done anything for me (clearly). I did my best to roll the thing back up. This story should really come with an unrolled condom so that you might experience my frustration, I got it about half way, very unevenly rolled, and couldn't take it any more. So I tried once again with a little more success to get it on and roll it down. It was about two thirds on, crooked and twisted. It was not comfortable, but it was the best I could do. My little friend was not pleased. Had he not been suffocated in latex, he probably would have advised me to go home and back to the drawing board. Screw that!

I paraded back down the hallway, nude but for the scroggled prophylactic, and slipped quietly into the room for the second act. She was lying on the bed just looking at me. What patience. She had put her shorts back on. I don't blame her. I wouldn't have been into sitting around alone in a relative stranger's house with my pants off. I said a simple "sorry," another fleeting instance of honesty, and we tried to resume with some sort of continuity, of which, of course, there was none. No change had occurred during my attempts at straightening out the mess I had made. Now, however, when I thought I'd be okay, staying straightened out was coming into question. This was definitely a new one on me. I didn't even try to figure it out. I just tried to work fast. Once again I could have told her what was going on and maybe she could have helped me out, or maybe, better yet, she might have concurred with my smallish partner and suggested trying another time. Instead, I plodded ahead. She seemed ready. It was now or never. It could have been now or twenty minutes from now. Jesus, we had all night to get it right. However, I didn't know about this phenomenon of loss and retention of readiness, especially when condoms are involved. It was another touchy subject we hadn't discussed.

The final issue which we had, or at least I had neglected (maybe Steve hadn't thought anybody who could speak as boastfully as I had could in reality be that lost) was insertion. I guess I assumed that nature was perfect in its ability to make things go smoothly when hormones took over our lives. It was blind faith. So, with blind faith I lay on top of her and moved around and tried to get us together and engaged, but for the life of me I could not make it happen. We just kept sliding around in random patterns with little glimpses of hopeful contact in the right regions, but no substantial progress. I really would like to see a transcription of her thoughts. And of mine. I stopped, reached down and tried to get some sort of reading of what I was dealing with. She was very expanded. Jesus, how could I miss? It gave me some fleeting confidence and again I tried to work things out through angulations and aimed thrusts. No such luck.

It finally occurred to me that I could find it beautifully with my hand, and I could definitely find myself with my hand and, with my hand as a diplomat, I could probably get the two together. No way. That would have been too easy. Also, I could scarcely bring myself to touch my little dictator when I was alone, so there was no way I was going to manipulate it with her in the room. No, no, it was definitely necessary for her to stay in the room. Wait a minute, she has hands. She definitely has hands. Man does she have hands. Why isn't she helping? Has she not. . . . No, she definitely has. (She had, by the way.)

Eventually, after more fruitless grinding, she too realized she had hands and offered some assistance, finalized by an enthusiastic "There we go." I didn't even say thank you. It definitely felt nice though. Better than nice. Soft, warm, receptive. For about a minute and a half, everything made sense. Then the Trojan company interjected again. I had grown a bit due to the good feeling and now each little twist and unevenness caused by my rushed application was felt. She was enjoying herself, or at least acting well, but at the same time I was being increasingly pinched and constricted. This tends to happen a little bit with a condom anyway, but when it is put on unsmoothly, its proddings and pullings are much more than a little bothersome. I writhed a little unconventionally and she tried to move with me. Maybe she thought I was onto some exotic technique. Maybe I was. The uniqueness of it and the comedy of her getting into it was lost on me. In perfect movie-like fashion, everything came to a crescendo at once. She was into it. Again I should have thanked her. At the peak of things, I couldn't stop from letting out a little, "Ouch." She laughed at that, possibly thinking I was the hippest cat in town. I wasn't even sure I had ejaculated. I just pulled out, somewhat satisfied and mostly glad it was over. The only thing I cannot remember vividly is exactly what happened in the next couple of minutes. I don't remember holding her or not holding her. I don't remember any words or our physical orientation. For what is usually the most intimate moment, the one just after loss of control, when we realize we've lost it in the presence of another, I have no memory.

The next thing I remember was shrinking enough to take the thing off. It was messy. For the second time the device dictated that I leave the room to deal with it. I hurried off to the bathroom. I didn't really want to look. It wasn't that pleasing looking, and that seemed dichotomous with the great illusion I had created for the sex experience. Great thoughts versus nitty, gritty story of my life, my sex life at least.

I was relieved going to the bathroom. By no means jubilant or tenderly triumphant or contented, but definitely relieved. I tried to laugh a little at my shaky performance. The whole circus had probably been going on for about forty-five minutes. It seemed like we had been up there for hours. I had no idea what time it was or where my friend and his girl were. The laugh didn't last long. Once in the light, my eyes were drawn to my loins, the focal point of which was red and tired looking. The condom was still in my hand, having been there for about ten minutes after I had removed it. My eyes moved from its recent inhabitant to it and the fun really began. It had a huge split, about an inch long, and inside was indeterminable from outside. Holy shit! Holy shit! Oh Jesus. My heart raced again, not in a good way, I assure you. I had no idea what to do. I resisted the urge to run back into the room in a panic and tell her. Easy, easy. I washed it in the sink. I have no idea why. I tried to analyze exactly what had happened, when, at what point, as if that made a difference. Maybe I didn't even, no, no I'm pretty sure I did. Shit. How could this happen the first time. Shit.

I tried to calm down with fleeting success. I decided to wait and talk to Shari about it. I anticipated the worst but repressed thoughts of my ruination. The two things I had definitely heard in the sex-ed class were that if you drink and drive you die and if you do it without protection, you cause a pregnancy. I was surprised at how easily the message came back to me when it had a practical application in my life. I did nothing short of plead with God.

I went back to her, trying my best to appear like a good thing had just happened, and swallowing hard on morose prognostications. I had no thoughts whatsoever about second attempts. I didn't know what I wanted, except that I didn't want to go through any of that again and I wanted to be out of there. I was extremely nice to Shari, what a guy, but once again I don't remember anything we said to each other. I was stone cold sober. We didn't stay in the room or the house for long. I drove her home and tried to bury doom in affection. I stayed up all night.

The day after I "lost it," I felt totally agitated, cheated, confused, alone. Wonderful, just swell. My mind slowed down a little bit due to excessive use. The phenomenon that I really couldn't believe was that I had no interest in seeing my friends. I went to church with my family. A record of my thoughts there would have been an interesting document in guilt.

I knew I had to call her. We were supposed to go out that night. "No way" was how my mind responded to that prospect. I was exhausted enough that I skipped working out, which was then like the pope skipping Mass, and of course further fed my guilt. The clothes I had worn smelled like her. Previously it had been all I could do to resist breathing through them compulsively. Now I couldn't stomach the aroma. I finally slept in the afternoon, only to wake up feeling totally physically nasty. I don't ever even remember having a cold in high school before this. I called her to cancel our date. To call the conversation uncommunicative would be the understatement of the century. I still hadn't spoken with anybody about my ingravescent surety that I was a parent at this point. It probably would have made sense to talk to my co-conspirator, but again the no-way feeling ruled. I apologized glumly and said I really was spent, which was true. I think she already sensed a disproportionate downturn in my feelings about the relationship, because I already sensed panic in her voice. I tried with zero success to add some levity with flippant humor. The conversation ended with an inconclusive deflation. I didn't call her again for four days. What class. I think for a fleeting moment I thought I could just make the whole thing go away.

In the intervening time, too much had happened. I talked to old confidant Steve about the experience. When asked how it was, I said, to my own astonishment, "great!" I told him about the exploding prophylactic and he just said "shit" which didn't help. He must have felt my disappointment melded with consternation, but didn't push it. He tried to joke and I tried to laugh at his jokes.

Finally I called Shari and just tried to talk, not even about anything. It was awkward, like traversing back to square one. What the hell, I thought, this was supposed to make you closer. I didn't know how she felt, probably totally confused by me. I had lost my sense of humor, a shocking occurrence, as, until you lose it you aren't aware it can be lost. She wanted to see me. I balked. I told her I was really sick, which was more true than I realized, but this must have seemed thin, as I was still working and working out. Now I began to realize I was being, or at least appearing, horrible to her. I began to feel horrible about that too.

She called me the next day. She had made me cookies. Nobody had ever made me anything before. It was getting messy. I said she couldn't come today and made up some absurd reason. She was starting to hurt. I'm not much into hurting people and in my tired and heightened sensitive state I felt utterly base. I lay in bed and sweated. Totally soaked the sheets. And the blanket. What the hell is going on. Football starts in three weeks. Jesus, I have to pull myself together. Actually, I doubt if I thought that because I didn't even have the concept that I could be apart. I have to end this thing with her. I can't be thinking about it when football starts.

She called again and I didn't return her call. I didn't know how I felt about her. I certainly had no malice. I just felt like it was too much and would be when I was leading my team into the annals of high school sports history. Of course this too was flawed logic (as if the word logic could even be applied at this point) because every high school gridiron hero needs a girl waiting for him outside the locker room, right?

Maybe this last glimmer of hope for her brought to bear the fact that she might not have been the girl I wanted waiting for me. I hadn't given her a chance. I hadn't introduced her to my mom, or hung out with her friends and my friends, or done anything but go out at night with her when the summer breezes were blowing through my jeans. Also, now poised to conquer this town and its cliques, I also had some idiotic remnants of the idea that I wanted its girls too. I mean the more typical ones. Like the ones that my older brother brought home. I was saving my fool self for some abstract girl I had in mind who probably wasn't worth my saving. There was also the little detail that she didn't exist as far as I could see. Hell, it was a small town, I knew everybody. The only girl I had ever had a decent conversation with was the one with the cookies and the intensely adorable smile whose phone calls I was not returning. Steve couldn't believe I was thinking about turning her loose after she "came across" as he would say.

She called again, and despite my increasingly confused state, I surprised myself by surprising her. Before she could say much at all, I said, "Hey, those cookies aren't stale yet, are they" and she said with a little touch of biting woman anger, "Yes, as a matter of fact they are." I countered immediately with what I think she really wanted to hear, which was, "good, that's just the way I like them, can you come right over?"

She came right over and I met her at the door and munched a few very stale cookies just to be a man of my word. My mom was looming around the way mothers will when they want some inclusion and some information. I suddenly realized that she had never even met my parents, and more acutely my mother. I awkwardly introduced them, but only after she had already brightly said, "Hi Mrs. . . . !" I think my mom was taken aback that she wasn't waspy like most of the girls she had seen my friends interact with. Still, as she was with everybody, Mom was nice. Exceedingly nice. Too goddam nice. It was queer to me. She niced my mom right back. I felt very distant from the whole thing.

I went back to work the next day feeling absolutely awful. I procrastinated for another day and finally called her. I started with the sympathy rap, telling her I was really sick, not really believing it myself. Unfortunately that wasn't enough for her to be compelled to say, okay you're excused, I'm okay, do what you have to. No, she definitely needed more. She said she missed me. Great. She wanted to come over. I said I didn't think it was a good idea as she might catch something. Okay, then, she wanted to know what I was thinking about her. Um, well, I missed her too but . . . BUT!? But what?! I sensed panic and hurt and, man, talk about impending. Well, I uh, I uh, um, you know, um, I miss you but, um I'm really sick and football is coming up and, I, uh, I just, um. . . . you still there? She was silent, and I was wretched. Then she said the worst thing she could have said, almost pleadingly, jumping ahead, "What did I do wrong?" She might as well have put her foot through the line and stepped on my adam's apple. "What . . . nothing, nothing, no, you didn't do anything wrong. It's me. It's not you at all, it's me. . . ." Try to break up with anybody and tell them it's got nothing to do with them. "What are you saying, you don't want to see me any more?'' She was actually less shocked than I. I couldn't believe after night upon night of yearning for her, I was trying to make her go away. For some reason it seemed like the only option. "No, I don't mean that . . . I just mean for a while, I need to concentrate on other. . . . ''

She cut me off, "But what about. . . .'' Now I was speechless. Yeah, you jerk, what about that great intimate moment of fumbling? Are you going to put her through that and then dump her? You prick, I couldn't believe how quickly I had gone from triumph to misery, the physical and the emotional inextricable. Goddammit, this was not how the fine script in my head was written, how dare life add all these goddam subplots. Dammit. Maybe I was wrong. Maybe I do love her. How could I feel so horrible about this if I didn't? I think I'm going to pass out. I pleaded with her now, "I don't want to hurt you, I just need . . . can't we just take a rest for a while, She turned sad in an instant, "Well, can I still call you?'' Another foot to the neck. "Of course you can call me. I want you to call me, I just need a little time. . . .'' Of course this would have the effect of making me always expectant of having to deal with another such phone call. Then abruptly, she blurted, "I have to go.'' I was naive enough then to think, when she said that, that she actually did have somewhere to go, rather than seeing it as a grasp for some sort of control—like, you're ending this relationship, well, then, I'm ending this phone call. And like that, it was over. I felt some immediate relief, and then of course sheer drudgery and self-loathing.

My mom came home from work to find me on the couch for the third day running. Basically an intrepid woman, she showed a little consternation at the complete colorlessness of my face. Despite my protestations (yes, I still believed there couldn't be anything wrong), she made an appointment for me to see the family doctor the next day. I sweated another night away. My throat began to burn and I coughed up things that only Steven Spielberg has equalled since.

Could things get worse? Of course they could. The doctor quickly and effortlessly diagnosed that I had traded one lay for Mononucleosis. That was the way my guilty mind saw it anyway. How long does it last? Usually a month or more. No way! I'm scheduled to become a football star in two weeks.

The phone rang at around eleven-thirty that Saturday night. A few minutes later my father, a generally austere and directed man, wandered aimlessly into my room with a leering grin on his face and asked with a comic edge in his voice. "You haven't been doing anything you shouldn't, have you, my friend?" I sprang out of bed and walked down the hall to their room where I found my mom in bed, seemingly oblivious. "Hey, Mom, who's on the phone?" "Well, it was a girl." A girl calling me was indeed a fairly infrequent occurrence, but I resented that implication.

"She didn't say who she was?" I asked. She chortled "No." "What's so funny? What'd she say?" Suddenly my mother became animated, assuming a very wavering tone in her voice, "W-Well, she said, "I-Is Rich there?" Then she assumed her drama again, nearly falsetto, "And she said, 'I really need to talk to him,' and I said 'well you'll have to call tomorrow,' so she said, 'W-W-Well, j-j-just tell him I'm having his baby!!!'so I said, 'OK, I'll tell him, good night.' "

I think my parents' comic nature about the whole thing really actually helped me, although they made no further mention of the whole affair. I guess they either didn't know how to approach it or just considered it a little past laugh. I was deathly ill, couldn't sleep, worried sick with good reason, feeling mean toward the only girl I'd ever been intimate with.

I was at a point where I was forced either to laugh or cry and somehow, amazingly, I laughed. I actually laughed hilariously, working up the image of my father in my mind. I tried to escape into it. I based my laughter on the one ability that adolescence offers in a superior form, the ability to hope. I hoped that she wasn't with child. I hoped that her friends had called in vengeance. I hoped that big hairy life was just playing a big ugly joke on little hopeful me. I begged a God whose existence I was unsure of for some deals, some time, something, dammit.

I did make a quick recovery. My spleen wasn't swollen so I was able to play in the first game. I made a diving catch under the lights in the end zone on the last play of the first half. Then we lost to the eventual state champs by a point in the last minute. I collapsed on the field at the end of the game and watched steam come off my chest. It would have been frightening if I had had any energy left with which to be scared. We had a good season and I had a good season, getting some recognition and even some attention from college coaches. I went to college where I learned that neither football not sex could really solve anything or offer the kind of apocalyptic moments for which I had been searching. Still, it took a long time before I stopped thinking about that first mono-influenced game; what if I hadn't been so sick so close to the season? Could I have produced one more burst of energy to break one more tackle. . . .

In retrospect, it isn't the game that I regret. I regret the fact that I had to go to such extremes to become aware of the most basic gifts of life. I actually endangered my health, both physical and mental, because of my desire for more, more, more, faster, faster, faster. I don't mean to knock the desire for experience and great moments, but I entirely took for granted the excellence of simply being young and alive and surrounded by friends. My blinders limited my breadth of vision so much that I did miss certain opportunities, mostly those provided by the voices of other people with other perspectives. Perhaps there is no use in playing "the grass is always greener." My absolutism toward things probably helped me to achieve a lot. Still, for a brief period when I thought I would be sailing, I was crawling with all my might, paying pretty hard for my narrow mindedness. I had pondered long upon how events should occur and almost completely neglected the practical aspects of living my life. It was probably the first time that my big and glorious plans for things clashed entirely with reality, and I was thrown hard.

All else aside, the loss of my virginity was an incredible lesson. I probably have a lot in common with a lot of people, if perhaps in more extreme measures. I may have more in common with women than most men, as many women have described the experience as painful, and then relieving when over, and then empty and very disappointing. I think the real pain involved was the pain of a near miss. Here was a girl who was available to me, open emotionally and physically. I could have learned so much from her and perhaps she from me. We easily could have been in love. We definitely could have had great sex. I was so encumbered by trying to uphold an image and so intensely focussed on my deluded dreams of glory that I couldn't get close. I think I stopped us from communicating, and ultimately that is the value of sexuality. It is a fantastic mode of communication.

There was also the issue of communication with my friends. Even with my closest friends, I valiantly preserved an image of near-stoicism to protect myself. If only I could have been honest, I might have gained some real strength, not to mention some more kindred spirits. I mentioned that it seems the only times that people speak openly with each other in the face of romance is in the movies. I think this is also the case with teenaged peers in movies who get pushed to the point of 'telling it like it is.' I think what really happens is that writers look back and write scripts in which the characters say, at the crucial moments, what the author wished he had said. Perhaps this is an instance where life should imitate art more often.

So, was she pregnant? I'll leave you to wonder as I did for some time. The point is that either way the question was traumatic due to the communication gap. If she was pregnant, you can imagine what I, and we, had to go through. Planned Parenthood is a great thing to support, but I assure you it's the last place you want to visit at the age of sixteen or seventeen. It is worse if you can't even talk to the one other person who knows. If she wasn't pregnant, then she very well could have been. Surely the knowledge of a negative answer would be relieving, but in this case the relief couldn't be shared. The lack of communication would still leave questions, pain and emptiness.

Can I laugh about it now? I can laugh at the ridiculous bedroom scene. I can laugh at the uncanny coexistence of my great visions and my utter mechanical ineptitude. I can laugh at my usually dour parents' improvisational vaudeville at my expense. What I really hope, though, is that she can laugh about it, and I have my doubts. Boys can learn so much from their female peers in the sexual realm, yet they often refuse to do so. I was, if there ever was one, the prototypical example. Self-damning, I have come to learn from years of trying it, is of almost no value, and so I chalk this experience up to learning, plodding along as well as possible without a manual. Still, I hope at least she can laugh at me, because I definitely deserve it.

13

The Same Little Girl from New England

by Anna Magdelena

"Are you a virgin?" I asked Steve, a high school summer boyfriend. He reacted as though I had asked him his feelings about barnyard animals. He look at me in disbelief and blinked seven or eight times, rolled over on his back and stared at the ceiling. "I wouldn't have asked the question that way. I would have asked if I'd ever slept with anyone," he replied. Figures. I used uncool terminology. I had asked the question wrong.

Virginity was a strange topic to me during my high school years. Prior to boarding school I went to a provincial day school in a small city for ten years where the theme of sex was bantered constantly about, but no one was actually having sex. Granted, 9th grade was my last year there, but even among the upperclassmen it wasn't apparent, or a way of life—possibly because I only saw them at school—but culturally it didn't pervade my sphere as a reality.

Suddenly I landed at a very cosmopolitan school where sex was an integral part of the social structure. As tenth graders, several of my classmates who were "cool" had upper-class boyfriends whom they were sleeping with. As time progressed, the percentage of friends who regularly slept with their boyfriends increased. Birth control was available through the infirmary without parental notification; STDs were less of a risk at that time and in that environment, and sleeping with one's lover at a boarding school was extremely easy.

I was not among those who were "cool." I arrived in this setting having spent most of my life working to get into prep school and playing Bach fugues. I was not chic as were many of the New Yorkers and Californians, nor as savvy socially, and was completely intimidated by the older boys. I wanted desperately to be cool, but didn't have the tools to pull it off. Also, I didn't regard myself as sexually attractive, particularly when compared with many of my classmates. Rather, I played the role of an insecure, square, New Englandy classical pianist. Additionally, after a day of academic rigor, hell at sports practice, seated dinner, chorus, madrigal singers, and homework, nothing was more alluring than sleep. I had consciously or subconsciously accepted that sex was simply not going to be an ingredient of my existence.

Never did I tangle with feelings of "God, my parents would DIE!" because when it came to issues involving sex, they were surprisingly laid back and supportive. My poker-faced father relegated these things to my not-even-remotely-poker-faced mother. For example, one morning during the previously mentioned summer, I was sitting at the kitchen table concentrating on pushing my Chex cereal into the bowl (so that the milk would eke out the squares) and absently asked "Hey, Mom, can I ask you something?" She abandoned the eggs frying on the stove, stole over to the chair next to me, clasped my hands in hers, looked understanding and said, "You and Steve made love last night. It's OK. Do you want to talk about it?" I had wanted to borrow the station wagon, and was almost embarrassed that I HADN'T been sleeping with Steve, or at that point even considered it, and that my question was so banal. She wasn't encouraging it, but accepting it as a rite of passage her daughter might have experienced. Further, I am several years younger than my older sister, so both parents were more relaxed about adolescent rites-of-passage than many other parents I knew.

My senior year during a vacation at home, I went to an internist for a check-up. The young, male doctor asked if I would like him to do a pap smear, and I reasoned that he probably ought to since I hadn't been to a gynecologist. Feet in the stirrups (yikes, they're chilly), uncomfortable drafts wafted up under the draping.

"OKOKOKOKOKOK, Anna, it's not THAT weird. Just grow up and DEAL," I kept repeating to myself.

"Hey, Anna, could you please relax a little, It won't hurt."

After several more attempts at trying to get me to relax, the doctor sheepishly explained that it probably wasn't worth the trouble since I was clearly a virgin.

"Didn't you even have any run-ins at prep school?" he asked in disbelief as I was getting ready to leave the office. Now I began wondering what the hell was wrong with me. Why wasn't I desperate to sleep with every male I knew? I was getting the impression that that's what normal seventeen-year-old girls were meant to do.

Freshman year at college. Wow! So many people, it seemed so huge (It was a small New England university). Everybody seemed artistic and interesting. I had arrived to study music and relax a little after what I felt was a too-rigorous high school experience. Prior to college I had smoked pot, smoked cigarettes fairly regularly, had been drunk many times, and seen *The Grateful Dead* in concert. It was high time to get this LAST adolescent hurdle out of the way so I could start behaving like an adult and concentrate on my new, groovy college curriculum. By now, I was extremely curious. I liked boys a lot, and "everything but . . ." was great fun. But how the hell do you go about losing your virginity if the last thing you would ever do in your life is pick up a random person at a frat party?

I was furious with myself for not having slept with Steve. He was kind. I loved him. And now I would be free of my still-a-virgin anxiety.

So I concocted a plan. One of my closest friends was older, (at this point I had no romantic interest in Steve who had moved to Paris), went to a different University, and surely would be happy to oblige me this small favor. I would call and explain that I really needed to lose my virginity and wasn't even going to consider a fling with a stranger. Lord knows how long it would take until I started seeing someone I *liked*, and hell, we liked each other intensely. He was attractive, experienced, would be sweet, and would keep his mouth shut. Done deal.

It never came to that. Instead, I began dating a very good friend of mine. It became intense very quickly. As we were already close, we didn't have to spend large chunks of time getting to know each other. As it became clearer to me that I was going to sleep with him, I began distancing myself. Unlike so many of my peers, I was incapable of physical affection on a purely physical level. It seemed that my classmates were comfortable with short-lived flings, and I knew that for whatever reason I would not be able to stomach that. Because of my sense of self-preservation (some would say isolation), I knew that if I were to make love to Justin, it would (in my head) create an attachment I was not ready for. In fact, I wasn't sure I actually really wanted to be bound to ANYONE emotionally.

However, one evening, Justin gingerly approached the topic and asked if we could make love. While I lay on my back thinking, "C'mon, Anna, just *** DO IT. Don't be such a coward. You totally blew it last time, don't blow it again. . . .'' I nodded a half-hearted OK and then propped myself up on my elbow to watch Justin unroll a condom. What a totally indelicate, strange ritual putting on a rubber is. Was I meant to know how to do this? I clamped my eyes shut and prepared for entry. All I could envision was the doctor remarking, "Didn't you have any run-ins in prep school?" while wielding a giant, icy-cold speculum. After several attempts at getting me to relax, Justin kindly suggested we call it an evening as he didn't want to injure me, and I didn't look very eager. I felt badly for him, but was vaguely relieved that it could be put off a little longer as it didn't seem like it was going to be a great deal of fun.

Conveniently, that was the evening before Thanksgiving break. While at home, my mother recommended that (now that I was in college) perhaps I ought to see a gynecologist. So I went to Dr. Smithson's office for a diaphragm. I was sure I would pass out on the table and he would explain to me that I was physically improperly designed or something. But he was great. Nothing hurt. Everything was totally fine. And now Justin didn't have to use what I thought at the time was a "bizarre rubber."

The first weekend back at college, Justin and I went to spend the evening at his parent's house about an hour from campus. We had a very pleasant dinner, and after the parents retired we disappeared to the playroom above the garage to listen to music and drink Midori and orange juice. I had surreptitiously snuck into the bathroom on the way up and inserted my new diaphragm. We lowered the lights, put on "Terrapin Station" by *The Grateful Dead*, which I guess I thought was romantic, and crawled into a sleeping bag from a mound of sailing equipment stored in the playroom. Admittedly, I felt very adult using a diaphragm instead of an ordinary rubber which could be bought at any neighborhood convenience store in the country. By mentioning to Justin that I had just slipped in my new toy, I had acquiesced to another attempt at this ritual. We necked for hours generating a great deal of body heat in the down sleeping bag, so we took off our clothes and found ourselves in the familiar missionary position. Once again, I was bracing myself for entry—rather the way you prepare yourself to dive into an icy lake. Christ it hurt . . . I couldn't believe that THIS could ever be recreational, or wasn't somehow harmful. Just hang on a little longer and Justin would be through . . . think of the empire . . . and this fall's tennis team . . . and how old was Bobby Wier when he first got laid I wonder....

Suddenly someone began climbing the stairs to the playroom. Both Justin and I froze. From above me Justin yelled, "Dad, don't come up here." I was too scared, and horrified, to breathe. I could feel Justin's heart palpitating at an unhealthy rate. "Justin, I have to go to the office, the alarm has gone off. Here are the keys to the back door," and his father flung a set of keys up and over the top of the stairs which then skitted along the bare floor towards us. Justin looked down at the keys, then at me and started to laugh. I stared up at him and murmured, "My God, I am still alive but please hurry up," which he did. We're done!!! I was so thrilled that we were done I couldn't believe it. I sprang up from the wicker sofa only to realize I was leaving a trail behind me. "Oh my God, it comes OUT!?"

"Anna, you idiot. What did you think happened?" Justin asked in disbelief. I actually hadn't thought about what became of semen and spermicide when you were through. After prancing about in a victory dance, I smiled down at Justin in the dim green light of the receiver.

"Anna. You're a goddess. I just made love to a goddess."

Two days later, I sat on the edge of my unmade bed in my room at college with the phone cupped under my chin listening to an endless stream of rings.

"Oh, be home, be home, be home," I muttered. Finally my mother picked up the telephone. I told her about psychology, my piano teacher, the plot of a book I was reading, how I had reorganized the shoes in my closet, and that I had lost my virginity.

"Don't worry, dear, it gets better," was all she said. And she was right.

Justin and I remained a couple for two years during which I became acclimated to the act of love making and found it enjoyable very soon after. I was lucky that my first lover was someone to whom I was very close. Now that I am in my late twenties and this all seems like a series of cartoon images from a past existence, I am embarrassed by the fact that losing my virginity represented such an obstacle. Adulthood is only a legal term. After enduring heartbreak, death of friends and family, financial insecurity, and the daily trials of life itself, the act of losing one's virginity seems like it ought to be as insignificant as taking a driver's test. Any and all growing up I did took place long after I first made love to Justin. But despite the passage of time and this alleged growing, I am still the same little girl from New England who seeks solace in Bach fugues.

14

What My Parents Didn't Tell Me

by Sybil Joy

Growing up in a conservative Asian family, sex was not a subject that passed frequently in conversation between parents and children. In fact, the taboo nature of the subject was so well understood that neither my sister nor I ever ventured to ask my parents where babies came from. So they never had to confront this uneasy subject by buying us books with tame illustrations or by resorting to the stork story. They just assumed we would find out sooner or later. And so we did, but through classmates and friends who didn't really seem all that knowledgeable either. How could they be? We were all virgins. In school, the teachers gave only the text-book, cut-and-dry explanations that removed all emotional factors. So along with preparing for the SAT's and college applications, I learned that women lose their virginity when the hymen, that thin mucous membrane covering part of the opening of the vagina, is ruptured by the penis during sexual intercourse. Often there is a slight bleeding when this occurs.

On the rare occasion that my mother did mention anything about sex, it was only on the topic of virginity. Virginity was something precious that was shed like the "pupa's cocoon" on the marital bed. Whereas the "pupa" turns into a miraculous butterfly, you turn into a woman, and then all the mysteries of adulthood are revealed. But if you were too hasty, foolish enough to give up your treasure too easily for immediate pleasure, or fall victim to the guiles of a smooth operator, you would suffer the consequences: unwanted pregnancies and failed relationships. Written off by society as "too loose," how would it be possible to find true love? Never mind true love, how could you find anyone to respect you? How could anyone do so when you displayed such poor judgment in tossing away something that important so quickly?

What could I expect from a mother who thinks "Looking for Mr. Goodbar" is a moral message to all those who participated in the decadent sexual revolution of the 1960's? At one point she made the analogy: losing your virginity before marriage is like being a used car—simply an object to satisfy immediate needs, nothing to be put on a pedestal, nothing to be cherished or loved. Virgins are pure, kind, beautiful, clear-skinned; married non-virgins are mothers; mothers are good, kind, generous, brave; unmarried non-virgins are selfish, cheap, loud, bad-skinned. What your parents say affects you, like it or not; you have no control over it. Words spoken when you are as young as six somehow find their way into your head to stay.

As a woman I was unknowingly bestowed with wonderful "potential." My sister was the pretty one in the family so being a virgin "with personality" was the one quality I had to make me attractive to the opposite sex. I didn't even question why virginity was placed on such a high pedestal. All I knew was that "good girls" were virgins and "bad girls" were not. Only virgins were sacrificed to appease powerful gods; unicorns preferred virgins to non-virgins; Elizabeth I was the "Virgin Queen" for her devotion to the throne (even though everyone who reads a bit of history knows otherwise); the blessed Mother Mary was still a virgin even after giving birth to the Son of God himself. I used to read tales of maidens who would rather kill themselves than be ravaged in the days of olde. They held their self-respect so fiercely that they became legendary for their virtue. Virginity was serious business. With all this floating in my head, I envisioned my "first" time to be the climax of my being, the culmination of the special relationship between two people. There would be such emotion and fervor that my lover and I would be bonded forever from that moment on. After all, if this was such a precious treasure to be guarded at all times, nothing less was to be expected.

As serious a business as virginity was in this country, my mother's "used-car" analogy was tame compared to a documentary I once saw on PBS. It was about growing up sexually in a tribe in some far away Middle Eastern country. Fourteen-year-old girls were circumcised without anesthesia in order that their future husbands receive more pleasure from them. A young girl was shown wailing in pain as her mother and aunt held her down while an elder woman performed this ritual. In another clip they showed a wedding festival where the husband took his young bride into the wedding chamber after dinner. He soon emerged from a curtained doorway holding a bloodied handkerchief in the air for the rowdy wedding guests to see—proof of her virginity. In a removed voice the announcer then told me that if the handkerchief had been clean, that would be proof that the bride had been deceptive about her innocence granting her husband the right to beat her and marry another in retribution.

And so it was with these images in my head that I ventured out into the world. While in high school, I met this guy three years older than I. It surprised me that I actually had a boyfriend at that age.

Unfortunately, there is nothing much to say about my first time except that it was unexpected and unwanted. Despite the "no's" and the tears, my boyfriend decided he knew what was best for me and carried off my innocence. After all, he was three years older. The disturbing part of the whole event was not the fact that I may have been "date raped" because I was not a willing partner (I was more a confused partner), it was that I felt nothing. Nothing. I was shocked to feel something slip inside of me, but after that initial sensation, my body grew numb. This can't be happening to me. I thought about some of the old black and white movies I used to watch late at night, where the woman falls madly in love with the scoundrel hero after he embraces her with fire and passion. My "friend" did more than embrace, but there was no passion here.

The sex itself, all by itself, wasn't stunning, exhilarating, or even plain bad. (Was it true what they say about penis size? Or was I doing something wrong?) One minute we were kissing, the next I was crying (but I didn't know why). My boyfriend tried to cheer me up saying, "It's not a big deal." and "I love you anyway." Anyway? I considered myself lucky that he was at least my boyfriend. I thought that meant he would have some commitment to me. I ran the whole scenario over and over in my head, dissecting each and every word spoken, every breath sighed, every movement taken, and I always came to the same conclusion. I felt cheated. I didn't blame him. After all, he was my first boyfriend, and it was so nice to have someone like me. I felt guilty. I had been too scared to try harder to resist. But how could I have let it happen so easily? How could I have let it slip through my fingers without much of a fight? It had happened so fast. I always prided myself on being quite an independent high-schooler. I had all my goals set out, just waiting to begin my life in earnest. This was not in my master plan. Not yet, at least.

I was scared to think of leaving him because I thought I wouldn't be able to find commitment from anyone else now that I had "lost" it. He, on the other hand, thought it was great that he had been my "first." He felt responsible for making me more "worldly." But I didn't feel "worldly" or wiser. None of the mysteries of adulthood had been unveiled to me. I thought I must be going through all this the wrong way. I really didn't love him before, and I surely didn't fall madly in love with him after. In my mind, I was still a virgin.

Maybe something was wrong with me. Why didn't I get really excited? Were my expectations too high? So what exactly is an orgasm and what does it feel like? Did I have one and just didn't realize it? Does it really make a difference how you feel toward the person? I knew what his penis looked like, what it felt like. I knew when he wanted to have sex, how, and for how long. But the only thing I knew about myself then was that I was unhappy. I was simply "going through the motions." It excited me a bit whenever we got together, like a roller coaster ride, but I always left with such an empty feeling. The roller coaster wasn't special anymore; I had memorized the ride.

My virginity was lost for this? Not only did I not feel right, I had to worry about preventing pregnancy. I never thought I would see the day when I was happy to get my period. When I started to fail in high school because of the pressures from both the college entrance exams and this relationship, my gut told me to break it off. The first time I tried, my boyfriend reminded me he was the one who took my virginity. Didn't that mean anything? Or was I just some slut? Did I seriously think I was ever going to find another boyfriend now that someone else had had me first? He held his prize over my head. Thoughts of the bloody handkerchief raced back in my mind. I had a choice. I could either stay with him or grow to become a very lonely woman.

I made the right choice moving away for college. Now I had the time to figure out who I really was and what I was doing. In college I met a lot of free-thinkers, people who were openly discussing everything—EVERYTHING, including sex. I wanted to talk to someone about how I felt, or rather what I didn't feel. I was looking for relief. After much deliberation I finally disclosed that I was no longer a virgin. My friends didn't disappear as I feared; my reputation was still intact. They were astonished that I treated the matter as a huge stone around my neck. Why such a heavy weight? I remember two of my friends telling me they had lost theirs at fraternity parties where they didn't even remember the guy's name. It was almost as if it was only a kink in a Friday night routine. Instead of "call up friends, go to a fraternity, meet people, party, go home to bed," it was "call up friends, go to a fraternity, meet people, party, lose virginity, party, go home to bed." Yes, they agreed they had been a bit surprised it wasn't the big event everyone hyped it up to be, but the surprise was short-lived. One friend said that after her first experience, she and her partner just sat up and watched TV. I wondered why my friends weren't disturbed by the disappointment, the let-down, the apathy. They more or less viewed losing it as an inconvenience that everyone experiences growing up, not unlike losing your first tooth or getting your period. In fact, they were surprised that it bothered me as much as it did.

We are living in the 20th century, and these are the 90's! Was I just a hopeless romantic? No, definitely not. My heart might soar, but my feet are firm.

Sex was, indeed, a casual subject in college, no longer the uninvited guest of my home. In fact, it was so casual it was sometimes just a passing activity. Instead of breaking for lunch, people would break for sex, and no one would bat an eye. Why should you refrain from something that was perfectly natural just because the Moral Majority deemed it appropriate that only married couples indulge. After all, the desire to have sex is a natural instinct to perpetuate the species. There's nothing wrong with that. Sex is a celebration of the body. There's nothing wrong with that either. But did that mean it was okay to simply "go through the motions" without any strong feelings about whom you were doing it with? You can love sex and have sex without a relationship. But that gets boring. Often I would hear a friend mourn about the fact that even though she had great sex (and a warm blush to her cheeks), she would rather have great sex with someone special.

I had a someone but was still waiting for the big one to happen. If I only had a special someone that would enable me to understand what "great sex" was. My boyfriend was now far away and grew even farther with the changing seasons. In fact, he was so far away that my head cleared and I decided to end the relationship a couple of months later. I opened myself up to good friends and realized I had not changed for the worse and had nothing to feel guilty about. The guilt and anxiety I had felt from losing my virginity vanished. There was nothing wrong with me, I just hadn't been ready to lose my virginity back then. I hardly knew who I was. How could I be ready to give part of myself away when I didn't even know what I was giving away? Now I felt angry at my "boyfriend," angry he had tried to hold his conquest over my head to keep me from leaving. Was I going to kid myself into thinking I was the only one he slept with when we were going out? And dare I think I was even "good?" How could I have been when my heart wasn't in it, when I felt nothing?

I was even angrier when I finally realized what I had given up for him. I gave away time, time for myself. I gave away the time to be free of the responsibilities of birth control, time free from worry about the risks of pregnancy, of AIDS and other sexually transmitted diseases. I gave away the time I had to really get to know who I am, what I want, who I want and when I want it. I was realistic enough to know I might lose my virginity before marriage, but, at least, I wanted to make sure it was exactly what I wanted. Being single was certainly better than staying in this relationship even though I wasn't sure I would meet someone who would truly care for me. I eventually did, and that's when I truly lost my virginity.

15

Outercourse: A Pleasure-Oriented Model of Sexual Expression

by Beverly Whipple, PhD, RN, FAAN

The emphasis of this book, *Losing It: The Virginity Myth,* is on sexual intercourse. According to Webster (1977), virginity is "the quality or state of being virgin" and a virgin is "a person who has not had sexual intercourse" (p. 1307). This places an emphasis on penis/vagina and penis/anus as the focus of sexual expression. This focus is a goal-oriented approach to sexual expression and is the antithesis of a pleasure-oriented model of sexual expression.

According to Timmers et al. (1976), there are two commonly held views as to the goals of sexual expression and sexual experiences: the first is goal-directed and the second is pleasure or non-goal directed. The most common is the goal-directed view, which is the emphasis of this book. This view is analogous to climbing a flight of stairs. The first step is touch, which leads to the next step, kissing. Going up the stairs, the next steps are caressing, then vagina/penis contact, which leads to the final step of intercourse and orgasm. There is a goal that both or one partner has in mind, and that goal is orgasm. If the sexual experience does not lead to a fulfillment of the goal, then the individual or couple does not feel good about the sexual experience, although much pleasure may have been experienced.

An alternative view is pleasure or non-goal directed expression, which can be conceptualized as a circle. Each type of sexual expression is on the perimeter of the circle, and each expression is considered an end in itself. Whether the experience is kissing, self-touching, oral sex, holding hands, stroking a partner, hugging, manual sex, etc., each is an end in itself and each is satisfying to the couple. There is no need to have this form of sexual expression lead to any other form of sexual expression.

It was with the concept of pleasure-oriented sexual expression that Perry and Whipple (1981) listened to what women described as pleasurable to them. Listening to the reports of women led to the rediscovery of a sexually sensitive area felt through the vagina, that they called the Grafenberg spot or "G spot." In presenting their findings in *The G Spot*, Ladas, Whipple and Perry (1982) emphasized that they did not want to see the G spot set up as a new goal. They state that "sex is for pleasure, and when it becomes goal-oriented, the pleasure is often diminished. The facts we have presented indicate that there are many dimensions to the way people experience sexual orgasm" (p. 170).

Although society has socialized people to be goal-oriented, with the concern for sexually transmitted diseases and AIDS, the alternative approach of pleasure-oriented sexual expression needs to be emphasized. Whipple and Ogden (1989) did just this in *Safe Encounters*. They emphasized that the whole body can be sexual. They gave many examples of how people can enjoy sexual pleasure from outercourse; behaviors that do not involve the exchange of body fluids. Outercourse emphasizes safe sex behaviors that provide sexual pleasure. Whipple and Ogden (1989) offer an extragenital matrix to help people map their body to discover which kinds of touch feel pleasurable to each part of their body.

Each person is a unique individual and as such, each person has the capability of responding sexually in a variety of ways. People have the potential to experience sexual pleasure from their thoughts, feelings, beliefs, fantasies and dreams as well as from physical stimulation. Whipple, Ogden and Komisaruk (1992) documented the report of pleasure and orgasm from imagery alone in the laboratory. They measured heart rate, blood pressure, pupil diameter, and pain and tactile thresholds in women who had an orgasm from genital self-stimulation and an orgasm from imagery alone, without touching any part of their body. In these women, there were no significant differences in the increases in the physiological and perceptual correlates of orgasm from genital self-stimulation and from imagery alone.

Sexual pleasure and even orgasm can be enjoyed without the goal-oriented approach of intercourse. There is much more to sexual experiences than penis/vagina and penis/anus contact. In this age of AIDS, society needs to encourage pleasure-oriented sexual expression. Men and women have to be aware of what is pleasurable to them, acknowledge this to themselves and then communicate what they find pleasurable to their partners. People need to be encouraged not to set intercourse, the G spot, or multiple orgasm as a goal that they must achieve. By focusing on a goal, they will miss much pleasure along the way. People need to be encouraged to focus on the process of sexual interactions rather than a goal and to enjoy pleasurable experiences.

References

Ladas, A., Whipple, B., & Perry J. (1982). *The G Spot: And Other Recent Discoveries About Human Sexuality.* New York: Holt, Rhinehart and Winston.

Merriam-Webster (1977). *Webster's New Collegiate Dictionary.* Springfield, MA: G & C. Merriam Co.

Perry, J.D., & Whipple, B. (1981). "Pelvic Muscle Strength of Female Ejaculators: Evidence in Support of a New Theory of Orgasm." *The Journal of Sex Research*, 17, 22–39.

Timmers, et al., (1976). "Treating Goal-directed Intimacy." *Social Work*, 401–402.

Whipple, B. & Ogden, G. (1989). *Safe Encounters: How Women Can Say Yes to Pleasure and No to Unsafe Sex.* New York: McGraw-Hill.

Whipple, B., Ogden, G., & Komisaruk, B.R. (1992). " Physiological Correlates of Imagery Induced Orgasm in Women." *Archives of Sexual Behavior*, 21(2), 121–133.

16

Pump!

by Charlie Cripton

I remember laughing as I drove home drunk from her house. I was alone in the car, but somehow it seemed funny. What made me laugh? I told myself I laughed because of how she had led me through it, like a whore who learned in the same pornographic texts my friends and I had first studied in fifth grade. But looking back, I wonder if perhaps I was laughing at the very fact that I had done *it* and my laughter was a sigh of relief.

It was a summer night. I had the sun roof of my Rabbit open to the moon, and my blood coursed, alcohol laden, through my veins. I drove through serpentine, suburban roads lined with mail boxes, maple and elm trees, and post and rail fences. The night fell into a sudden cool, and there was no thunder except of the crickets and cicadas in loud chorus.

I laughed as I drove along, laughed at how she'd kept coaxing me, and how it seemed as though she were using a pornographic novel as her guide. "Pump it. Oh, yeah, keep pumping it. That's it." Seriously? Did she really say that? My friends would want to know. Yes, I would be able to avow, she did indeed say it. I wanted to be excited by her attempts at sexiness, but I didn't believe her. I had to bite my tongue to keep from laughing the whole time we were together. And now I laughed, partly in jubilation and partly at her daring attempts at sophistication.

"Pump it," she'd said. What a strange imperative. No one from my side of the tracks at 16 would have dared speak such words with such carelessness with a drunken boy who one had only just met. "Pump it," she'd said. What did it mean?

We weren't talking about bicycle tires or light sweet crude. We were talking the proverbial *it,* the snake slithering with the knowledge of good and evil in its head into Eden.

It sounded silly, but her unintentional allusions to pneumatic pressure and oil rigs were apt; there was something mechanical and heartless about it. I don't think either of us even enjoyed the process more than workers on a derrick. And I am glad not to have been a woman, losing her virginity in such a way to a man who would have chanted "pump it" and held complete sway over me, a drunken woman. It has always seemed that men, or boys, are less exposed. They are the guests, the woman the host, and in the best of all possible worlds, she is entirely willing. If I had been a woman, I don't think I'd have been willing to lose it the way I did: drunk, dead drunk, and to a stranger without protection from disease or pregnancy.

But as a young man, I didn't care. Ripeness was all. Was she pretty and was she eager? Why yes, she was, and away we pumped, pumped deep into the night into the Earth's central core where the molten magma runs and the plates of rock collide ever so slowly and spew forth the lava that erupts. Yes, she was pretty and eager, and I drunk and not in love at all. Mostly what was on my mind was whether our pelvic collision would be interrupted by an irate, rifle-wielding Catholic father with a flaming red bald patch on top of his head. The goal was to make it in and out before he came down the stairs.

That bald man's daughter and I met at a party in someone else's house one summer. It must have been July. A friend and I made sexual exploits with random girls our top priority that summer. My friend, who compensated for my shyness, dubbed us the suburban cowboys. "The suburban cowboys ride again!" he would holler whenever we saddled up his Honda Civic to head out to whichever bar would accept our fake ID's. He would want to know, "Did you get your dick wet?" as he would yowl in his pseudo cowboy grunt. "Yes," I would be able to say, "Not only did I get it wet, I *pumped it.* I was commanded to."

The party where I met her took place at a house where the parents were out or didn't seem to care what went on. I arrived with a good head of steam and a flask of Jack Daniel's sour mash whiskey I'd procured at a liquor store in a nearby ghetto area.

Cathy, for that was her name, approached me smiling. That's all I remember. She was blond and well shaped, her teeth perfect. Her eyes, I suppose, were blue. That was enough, so I smiled back. That was all I could perceive through the sour mash veil I wore over my eyes. She seemed the life of a party at which I knew no one. Soon when she passed me she pinched and squeezed me and chuckled. Then somehow, I offered from the haze to drive her home. She seemed already to have laid out plans. It was all so easy; I was only the co-pilot on a first run. It was almost as though I didn't have to ask her. It had been assumed by her winks and pinches that the evening would unfold that way. Never had there been any doubt in her mind, and never did I have to ask anything. I only had to wait and sip on my sour mash and beers that were at hand.

Other people who had arrived with me at the party found alternate transportation home. She slipped into my car. I did, too, not giving a thought to my drunkenness. It was just the two of us. She must have known what she wanted to, and could, do. I was hers. She was 16, Catholic, and more sexually experienced; I was a shy Anglican, late in puberty, and a student at a prep school where hockey jocks and lacrosse studs stole the girls.

Cathy lived on a quiet cul de sac—a typical suburban setting lined with boxy, two-story houses in the colonial style on quarter-acre plots with pools behind them. She told me to drop her off, then circle around and park the car up the street and wait for her on her front lawn. She said she'd go inside, then come back out and get me. I guess maybe she kissed me in the car. I can't remember, and it doesn't matter.

As I lay on her front lawn in the suburban stillness, I felt like a soldier in a trench, hunkering down. No lights shone. I remember later she said her father was an executive at a chain saw company. She said the company's name as though of course I would have heard of it, and I had, but only vaguely. It was nothing much compared to the Blue Chip where my father worked, but I happened to have a job that summer involving clearing brush and forest and using a chain saw. She was a sailing teacher at a local yacht club. But that night I did not know any of these things about her, and I would never learn much more.

Before too long she came out and led me around the back to the steel cellar doors of her house. One was propped open, and we descended. Inside was a comfortable basement with simulated woodgrain panels, shag carpets, a wide screen television and bean bag chairs. She led me by the hand.

"Take off your clothes," she said. Wasn't that supposed to be my line? Well fortunately, she had more guts, so it didn't have to be, and it never has been since. "Oh, okay," I said. Was it a physical? Would I have to turn my head to the side and cough as some antiseptic nurse jabbed a cruel index finger into my crotch?

I took off my T-shirt, blue jeans and boxer shorts. She removed her tank top and skirt. She grabbed *it* and started to lead *me* by *it* across the room to one of the bean bag chairs where she lay down and brought me into her. I remember asking, "Don't we need something?"

"No" she said. "Just pull out before you finish."

It took some fumbling, but it went inside as easily as we'd slipped into her basement. *I made it!* I thought. *So this is what it's like! I've done it.*

I kissed her mouth, plunging towards her tonsils with my tongue as she did with me. Victory was mine.

But there was more. "Now you've just got to pump it," she instructed. "There, that's it. Keep pumping it." And so it continued until the life creating liquid was about to be transferred into her. I pulled out, and spilled myself onto her.

She was happy, and we hurriedly dressed. I wanted to kiss her. I kissed her and left, maybe getting her telephone number on the way out. We saw each other and did it again one more time, maybe twice. We went to a dance at a yacht club together. It was getting romantic. I remember seeing her beautiful body in a bikini in their swimming pool once when I visited during the day. She was svelte. Her beasts were small, and perfectly round. Her stomach and haunches also left nothing to be desired. She was centerfold material and willing to consort with a lowly 17 year-old male whose body had received just barely enough testosterone to be able to perform the act.

I remember once when we did it, she showed no concern for her own pleasure. And when she didn't notice that I had taken my pleasure and she assumed I hadn't, she was disappointed. "That's never happened to me before," she said. It was as though she was eager for the knowledge of good and evil, pleasure and pain, eager to confront age and all its disappointments head-on. She even wanted to experience a man's impotence, a treat usually reserved for much older women.

Clearly, this was a woman with a mission. She had something to prove, and in that respect, we were equals. Our missions differed, though. Hers was to show she could seduce and give pleasure to any man. Mine was to go where all real men have gone before.

I've often thought, perhaps incorrectly, that her religious background, with its relentless confessionals and emphasis on chastity, had something to do with her mission. She attended a parochial school and church, no doubt. Maybe at her school, the name of which contained the word "convent," she was a famed seducer of the entire football squad.

That kind of thought collided with the discovery of the herpes epidemic. *Could she have it? Have I got it now?* I waited and waited and nothing happened, so I guess not. But I later ran into a friend who had lived across the street from her and who claimed to have made it with her several times. He said most people had.

My mission that summer was to drive in the spurs of the suburban cowboy, to ride the horse of summer debauchery into experience. Pleasure did not count as much as achievement. It was a by-product never spoken of.

As I try to recall that incident amid the bean bag chairs and burnt-orange shag carpet fibers, I am bothered more by what I cannot recall than what I can. But of what I can recall, I wish that somehow I could have known more what I was doing. The suburban cowboys rode again, indeed. "Did you get your dick wet?" my friend asked. The question exposed the secret: It wasn't really so much about sex or love or romance as it was about whatever we had done at age seven—capturing the flag, kicking the can, tagging someone with a flashlight beam. Sex was a game we took up, a grown-up's activity we made a child's.

17

The Game

by Connie Maple

During my junior year in high school I came to the conclusion that I was sexually attracted to women. The concept was still somewhat new to me. I had not yet identified myself as a lesbian. In fact, I was not too certain of my sexuality in general. Having recently experienced hostility from my family at my explorations in same-sex attractions, I was reluctant to trespass beyond the frontier of curiosity.

Nonetheless, I had decided that to become a *bona fide* woman-loving woman, I had to have a sexual experience. I did not understand why I believed this. Most of my presumed heterosexual friends were virgins. Yet, they did not have to "prove" their sexual identity. Why should I?

In the summer before my senior year in high school, I met a woman named Rebecca. She was a senior in college and was in New York visiting. I found her to be an interesting and intelligent person. Initially, she did not strike me as a woman in whom I would be interested. However, she was to be the first woman with whom I would have sexual relations.

I knew that I wanted to experiment in my sexuality. My mother had told me she felt that what two women do together in bed was absolutely disgusting, although she couldn't really imagine what they could do. She said it was "understandable for me to have a strong bond with another woman." However, falling in love with a woman was not acceptable. Making genital contact with another woman was "repulsive, unnatural." Somehow I knew her argument was flawed.

When I first met Rebecca, I did not immediately fall in love with her. I saw her again when I went out of town to visit Sam, a mutual friend of ours, at his college. While Sam was busy, I spent time with Rebecca to get to know her. I learned how fascinating she was; we had wonderful conversations and spoke about issues which were of mutual importance to us. I did now recognize the attraction I felt toward her.

Unfortunately, my stay was not as blissful as I would have liked as I encountered family turmoil. I was in Rebecca's room when Sam called to inform me that my mother had called and wanted me to call her back immediately.

I used Rebecca's phone to make a collect call to my mother. Our conversation turned into a fight. I did not want to argue in front of Rebecca because the whole situation was embarrassing. On the other hand, I could not let my mother pummel me with a ridiculous monologue. At least I had to dispute what she was saying.

After I hung up the phone, I ended up describing my living situation to Rebecca. She then opened up to me and told me about her background. We found many commonalities in our personal experiences. Our words became infused with honesty and intensity. We got better acquainted in those few hours than we could have in several days of casual meetings, such as the one we had at the restaurant in New York.

At the end of my visit, we exchanged addresses and phone numbers so we could stay in touch. A few weeks later, I called Rebecca and sent her some of my poetry. She loved my work and wanted me to send more. The next time I visited her, I saw my poetry lying open on her desk.

In November, I went to visit Sam again. After spending some time sharing experiences and relating what was currently going on in our lives, we went to his dining hall to meet his friends. While eating lunch I unexpectedly saw Rebecca enter with another woman. Rebecca looked incredibly attractive, radiating beauty, strength, and sensitivity. She was with a woman I had never seen before. I didn't know the nature of their relationship.

Eventually, Rebecca's friend, who was "just a friend," left. That gave me the perfect opportunity to speak to her. I went over and started to inquire about her life and tell her about mine. We were happy to see each other. Again, we engaged in a soul-searching conversation. Something traumatic was going on in both of our lives. We discussed these important issues.

We talked so long that Sam and his friends left. In fact, we stayed until the dining hall workers were about to shut down the dining hall when we realized we were alone. We didn't want to end our penetrating, emotionally charged conversation.

As we realized that we needed to leave, we discussed our plans for the evening. Rebecca intended to go to a dinner party that a political organization with which she was associated was hosting. She invited me to accompany her and to a party afterwards a friend of hers was throwing.

Since there were a couple of hours before the reception, we decided to walk about the campus. The ambiance was romantic. When I started to get cold, we chose to go to Sam's room to put on some warmer clothing. After I changed, we sat in the dark on the sofa and continued to talk and relax in the comfortable intermittent silences. I showed Rebecca an infamous editorial on gay rights that I had written for the school newspaper, of which I was the co-editor.

We went to the reception. At this point, I had begun to feel extremely comfortable around Rebecca. I wasn't following the main discussions, which primarily concerned state politics. As I imbibed more shangrila, the warm feelings I had previously experienced turned into tingling sensations.

The assemblage of all these political minds bored Rebecca and me, primarily me. So, we left after having gorged ourselves on a hefty amount of free popcorn and drinks and decided to postpone the next party until later in the evening. In the interim, we needed something to do. I suggested we wait in Rebecca's room.

Rebecca thought my suggestion was fabulous. We went to her single room. Somehow we did not make it to the party. An electric field sizzled any notion of leaving the room before dawn.

There was nowhere to sit except on her bed. I positioned myself against the wall near the window. Rebecca leaned against the intersecting wall. We talked for a half hour or so and listened to "Sweet Honey in the Rock."

I took off my shoes, and Rebecca commented on my feet. I then moved one foot to her lap, where she began to caress it. We were both getting excited and had gradually stopped talking. Our mutual attraction had surfaced in a grand way. Our words ebbed, while our sexual sensations for each other were proportionally aroused.

In the middle of one of our cadenced pauses, Rebecca said, "I'm really attracted to you." What ensued was my first sexual experience.

I was relieved that Rebecca was more experienced than I. She gently and sensitively told me what stimulated her. She asked what I wanted. Unfortunately, I was too nervous to derive as much satisfaction from the experience as I could have. Whatever she did felt wonderful enough. I made no special requests.

The next morning I felt stranded. She was in a deep sleep, and I was uncompromisingly awake. I must have lain glaring at the ceiling for an hour or two. Not knowing what else to do, I just looked around some and twitched as much as possible without disturbing Rebecca.

Eventually she woke up. We got dressed and went out to pick up a paper and some coffee. We didn't talk much the next morning. Later I left to go meet Sam. I told him my secret. "I had sex! I gleefully exclaimed. "It was great!"

As I sloughed off my initial sense of wonder and awe at having finally "done it," I noticed that I had some marks on my neck. I was shocked. "How could they have gotten there?" I naively asked. After having thought about it, I decided that I liked having hickeys. The symbolism excited me. They marked my first sexual encounter. They branded me as a woman-loving woman.

Once I got home, however, I realized that having marks on my neck was not entirely positive. I did not live with my parents any more, so I didn't have to worry about the abuse that might have followed. I did have to find turtlenecks to hide the colored contusions at school. Unfortunately, I could not wear a turtleneck to basketball practice.

When I stepped on the court, I was instantly inundated with questions about the origins of the marks. Who was *he*? Where did I meet *him*? How long had I been going out with *him*? All these questions confused me. I was still glowing from the ecstasy. I wanted to relate my pleasure to my teammates, but felt deprived of that privilege. When they asked *his* name, I couldn't respond "Rebecca."

We had an away game the next day. On the way home on the bus, the questions started once again. I was able to avoid them on the court. I could just dribble somewhere else or shoot at another basket. On the bus, actually a van, I did not have the luxury of escape. I had to face the interrogation.

I had enjoyed myself too much to conceal the experience. So, I started to describe the *person* who had put the marks on my neck. I named Rebecca's age, school, area of study, and some physical characteristics. However, I had given away so much information that the next logical question, the one I had been avoiding all along, was bound to arise once again—what was *his* name?

I somehow managed to squeeze my way out of that situation. I might not have done so adeptly, but I saved myself from the ridicule that probably would have followed.

On that bus, I learned a lot. I learned that I could not tell these people what they wanted to hear. I also quickly saw the reinforcement of my inability to lie. Although I still lived a closeted life, I could not give Rebecca a masculine name.

Now that I self-identify as a lesbian and am out, I try to forget that experience. My joining together with a wonderful woman will always persist in my memory, but the session of interrogation fades.

I felt insecure about losing my virginity in general and even less confident of being sexual with another woman. The interrogation on the bus and on the basketball court crystallized my fears about being a lesbian. My greatest fear was always based on other people's ability or inability to understand me and the passion that I felt towards women. The label of lesbian devalued my emotions. The societal definition and implications did not measure up to my feelings. The encounter with my teammates reinforced my belief that others could not understand my natural proclivity toward women.

Now I wish I had been more powerful in my coming out period. I chastise myself for not having been able to tell my teammates that Rebecca was *her* name. I wish I could have said in a self-assured manner that we had not been lovers for three years before I decided to "give myself" to her. I would like to have said that we were friends who felt a sexual attraction for each other and wanted to act on that attraction.

I try to forget what happened during my first sexual encounter, because it is painful to remember how easily and stupidly I let myself fall in love. I subconsciously felt that I had to fall for whomever I had sex with. On a logical level, I understood that I could not date this woman, that we lived in different states and had different life plans. I knew I wasn't in love with her and didn't want to fall in love with her. Nevertheless, I felt compelled to "fall for her" in some manner despite our presexual agreement that nothing else would ensue.

Now I look back at the experience and feel embarrassed about my lack of sexual sophistication. I had been precocious in most of my academic and extracurricular activities. I was used to knowing what to do and how to do it in any aspect of my life. Yet, sexuality was an unknown domain for me.

I feel that my lack of knowledge about sex was related to my being a woman and a lesbian. As a woman, I was not socialized to explore my sexuality, to find out what I wanted and would enjoy in bed. I didn't even know where my clitoris was. Coming from a conservative and Southern family, I was taught that I would simply find the man of my dreams and get married.

As a lesbian, I had no models of sexuality. Every women's magazine cover I had read dealt with how men and women date and handle their sexuality. My first girlfriend and I, although we did not have sex, bought a book on lesbian sexuality to learn what to do and what roles sexuality had in various types of relationships. After my first sexual experience, I bought a more detailed book to learn specific techniques for love-making.

That first experience remains with me in my current relationships. I remember how upset I was when I had inflated my expectations for the relationship. Now I consider that hurt and attempt to reduce the expectations that I put on a new lover. I protect myself. I view sex as a positive experience that does not have to be based on love and does not have to be filled with intense meaning.

18

Reasons to Wait

*by Patrick F. Bassett, President
Independent School Association of the Central States*

The bombardment of images in the popular culture today are surely more weighted towards forsaking virginity for pleasure than for restraining oneself until adulthood or marriage. It is somewhat surprising and reassuring, consequently, to find a significant number of adolescents who maintain their virginity, despite considerable pressure to do otherwise. The most recent polls indicate that around 50% of those 17 or younger remain virgins. Once past seventeen, however, the figures change dramatically. Seventy-two percent of high school seniors, male and female, have experienced sexual intercourse (according to the Centers for Disease Control), but those that hold out until that point seem to have made a firm decision to remain chaste, since 25 percent of females still remain virgins at 19 (and 20% of never-married women remain chaste through their twenties, as reported by The Alan Guttmacher Institute) (Pagnozzi, 235). Research on teenage sexual activity shows that of those who plan to finish only "some of high school," 76% are nonvirgins; of those who plan to complete "all of college," 76% are virgins, the mirror opposite in numbers (Coles and Stokes, 203). Since the physical, emotional, and psychological dangers of early intercourse increase as one goes down the age scale (the younger you start, the more likely you are to have multiple partners and increased risks), a decision to abstain or postpone sexual intercourse is both wise and deserving of support.

If there are fundamental cultural, moral, and parental prohibitions against premature engagement in sexual intercourse, then what are the countervailing pressures that teenagers feel that override the inhibitors? Current popular media are of course one source of powerful persuaders. The advertising world (Calvin Klein ads in particular), television soaps, sitcoms, and the film industry present sex without commitment and consequence in highly telescoped relations in which the period from encounter to intercourse occurs in the blink of a camera's eye. One recent study revealed that over half of the teenagers polled indicated that the way sex and its consequences are shown on television is the way it is in real life (Howard, 75-6). Students who believe TV accounts of sex are accurate are more likely to be dissatisfied with their own first experiences (Haffner & Kelly, 31). Peer pressure is possibly the most potent contributor to premature sexual involvement: many studies show that significant numbers of adolescents have engaged in intercourse not because they themselves wanted to but because they felt their partner expected it of them, and they did not know how to refuse (Howard, 75-6). In today's entertainment landscape the question of whether or not to engage in teen sex is merely rhetorical (O'Connor, 15). Furthermore, the fictional presentation of the stages of sex leaves out crucial intervening steps: Doogie and Wanda in the TV sitcom "Doogie Howser, M.D." agonize for a polite period of time over the question of intercourse, kiss, grab the condoms (Doogie is a physician, after all, and safe sex is politically correct for the networks, if virginity is not), and jump into bed, giving the impression that seems universally assumed by too many teenagers: 1. That if there is a moral dimension to sexual intimacy, just hesitating is enough to show one's moral strength; 2. That if I do make a thoughtful decision to have sex, I will also be responsible and protect myself. 3. That the natural successor to kissing is intercourse.

Sex education in most school programs teaches the mechanics of human sexuality without the necessary warnings about not turning on the engine: the implicit message is that because you are of legal age to drive, it is fine to take the car around the block, even though no one has issued you the license or signalled a green light. Although few adults would argue that we should return to the days of general ignorance about human sexuality, increased familiarity with the mechanics of sexuality and the easy access to condoms in college dorm concession areas has demystified sex to the point of making it commonplace and, therefore, acceptable in the minds of most teenagers. Education is not the issue anymore so much as values and decision-making patterns, since we have completely inundated young people with warnings about teen pregnancy, STDs, and especially AIDS. Legislating deterrents as in the case of drugs and alcohol led to campaigns by schools and parents to change attitudes so that the "I choose NOT to use" attitude became acceptable. These same principles can apply to early sexual encounters.

The AIDS epidemic has dramatized the urgency to educate young people about the dangers of sexual encounters, but since only abstinence is completely safe, and since most teenage intercourse (between 50 and 90% according to different reports) is unprotected, health education falls largely on deaf ears.

What, then, is the kind of advice adults should be offering teenagers to enable a wise choice of virginity?

First: that virginity should be preserved for adulthood or marriage. . . depending on one's value system. Each of us would define adulthood differently: some by age (18 or 21), some by stage (out of high school and working or in college), some by level of independence ("You are not an adult until you pay your own way," or "the Golden Rule of parenting: he who holds the gold makes the rule"). Adulthood probably does not occur at 17 or younger, since rare is the teen who is capable of making all the judgments necessary to handle the commitment and consequences of sex at an earlier age.

Second: that there is a hierarchy of expressions of caring and love, steps and stages that evolve naturally, and that there is no need to rush to intercourse. . . as the final step, when there is plenty of time to arrive there eventually. Although parents and teachers often feel comfortable describing and diagramming the most intimate of genitalia since this clinical approach is non-threatening to all involved, it is the steps of intimacy we avoid that need much further exploration and explanation. We've come a long way from the attitude of 50 years ago when a young lady was chastised for permitting a particularly adventurous young man to place his hand over hers in the company of their chaperone with "Don't you think you should save *something* for marriage?" However, there are ways of talking, touching, caring, sharing that are very intimate but fall short of invasive, penetrating sexuality. This is the substance adults should be offering and adolescents seeking.

Third: that to choose virginity is to take pride in oneself and to manifest strength of character, despite what others may say. . . . One does not have to be a nerd "to choose not to use" alcohol or drugs, just as one does not have to be a prude to choose to abstain from sexual intercourse at too early an age. In fact, "the times, they are a-changing": there are encouraging signs that many students are choosing for a variety of reasons to abstain. Any friendship that is jeopardized by an abstinence choice needs repair work in the first place.

It has been my experience, and that of many of my colleagues, that when an adolescent seeks adult counsel about sexual experimentation, what the adolescent is most often seeking are ways to say "No." If an adolescent wishes validation to experiment, he or she would go to a peer. The fact of an adolescent's seeking out an adult on this difficult issue demands an adult response. If the first adults you turn to cannot be helpful with the abstinence or postponement decisions, find another adult. Loss of virginity, is just that, a loss you need not contend with given the proper communication and your own strong will.

Sources and Resources

Burkhart, Kathryn Watterson. *Growing into Love.* New York: G.P. Putnam's Sons, 1981.

Coles, Robert and Geoffrey Stokes. *Sex and the American Teenager.* New York: Harper's, 1985.

Francoeur, Robert T., Ed. *Taking Sides: Clashing Views on Controversial Issues in Human Sexuality.* Guilford, CT: The Dushkin Publishing Group, 1989.

Haffner, Debra and Marcy Kelly, "Adolescent Sexuality in the Media." SIECUS Report, March/April 1987. Excerpted in *Teenage Sexuality, Opposing Viewpoints,* David L. Bender and Bruno Leone, Series Editors. St. Paul, MN: Greenhaven Press, 1988.

Howard, Marion. *How to Help Your Teenager Postpone Sexual Involvement.* New York: The Continuum Publishing Co., 1991.

MacDonald, Donald Ian. "An Approach to the Problem of Teenage Pregnancy." *Public Health Reports,* July-August, 1987. Reprinted in *Teenage Sexuality, Opposing Viewpoints,* David L. Bender and Bruno Leone, Series Editors. St. Paul, MN: Greenhaven Press, 1988.

O'Connor, John J. "Critics Notebook: On Teenage Virginity, or Its Loss, On TV." *New York Times,* 09/21/91.

Orr, Lisa, editor. *Sexual Values: Opposing Viewpoints.* San Diego, CA: Greenhaven Press, 1989.

Pagnozzi, Amy. "Virgin With Attitude." *Glamour,* April, 1992.

Rodman, Hyman, Susan H. Lewis, and Saralyn B. Griffith. *The Sexual Rights of Adolescents.* New York: Columbia University Press, 1984. Excerpted in *Teenage Sexuality, Opposing Viewpoints,* David L. Bender and Bruno Leone, Series Editors. St. Paul, MN: Greenhaven Press, 1988.

19

Sweet 16

by Roxanne Connors

If my mother could have uttered the word "sex," I think my perceptions and preoccupations on the subject might have been quite different. A true product of the fifties, Mom doesn't even use the clinical word "pregnant" but says "she is having a baby." Needless to say, "sex" or any derivation of the word or topic was approached with such trepidation that her voice quivered when she tried to speak. At such moments, I responded like most of my friends and either ignored her or suggested she go lie down. Too embarrassed to pursue the topic, she, instead, handed me a primer on the reproductive system. That was about all I had for sex education.

At my school, St. Ann's, I did have an eighth grade health class where we were shown a film on the reproductive system. It proved only slightly more informative than my mother's inaudible utterances. Consisting of a cartoon in which sperm go in search of egg, the narrator discussed how the egg was fertilized and how a zygote developed into a baby while still inside the mother's womb.

Unfortunately, the narrator stopped there. For this classroom of prepubescent young girls there was no explanation of why or how a woman's body reacts or becomes aroused. There was no discussion of the physical act or the emotions involved before the miraculous process of fertilization began. More importantly, the film failed to describe or explain what happens to a man's and woman's body during the time of arousal. I was completely horrified to learn, one or two years later, that men became "hard."

I remember coming home after a two hour make out session wondering why I had stomach cramps. My first boyfriend, Paul, tried to sympathize but didn't know what was wrong either. He knew why he hurt. He described it as "blue balls" which sounded completely disgusting. I had a "stomach ache." That was all, nothing else. What I didn't know was that we were suffering from the same exact thing.

Neither had the film supplied any points of reference concerning make out strategy or what to do next. Or what we could do next? Or if we really wanted to do anything next.

I had met Paul the summer before my junior year in high school. We were both taking driver's education in a nearby town in northern Virginia. We didn't really meet until we painfully caught eyes when my younger brother shouted at me from the back seat of my mother's car, "HEY THAT'S PAUL THOMAS; HE WAS A COUNSELOR AT CAMP WHITEHALL." It turned out that Paul and my brother went to the same school, St. Andrew's, the brother school of St. Ann's. Driver's Ed class met every night for two weeks so we had no choice but to exchange at least a few words while waiting for our mothers to pick us up.

Paul and I quickly became friends and agreed to catch up when school started. Surprisingly, we bumped into each other about a week after the end of Driver's Ed. I was there to pick up my brother after football practice. Paul and I laughed together and seemed to have a lot to talk about. He played varsity football and appeared almost Adonis-like with only his football pads to cover his muscular upper body. I don't think I was swooning, but that was the closest I had ever been to a man's unclothed body. I remember thinking, "Get a hold of yourself, Roxanne." But I was impressed.

I didn't hear from Paul again until the beginning of October. He called to see if I had a date for the Homecoming dance, four weeks away. I did not, but told him I was unsure of whether I should go with him since we had never been out before. One could not go to such an important event without knowing the guy better than I knew him. I am not really sure where this rule of thumb came from, but I thought only real geeks would show up for big events with people they didn't really know. Secretly, of course, I was thrilled because I dreaded the approach of Homecoming season, had never had a date to this event before, and probably had a slim chance of getting one since I knew so few people at St. Andrew's. I, therefore, suggested we go out before, and decided I could be free the following weekend.

The Homecoming Dance was very exciting. First we went to dinner at the Fort McNair Officer's Club, where Paul seemed somewhat depressed since our team had lost the game earlier that day and not much I could say would cheer him up. But he was trying his best despite the loss. He had brought me flowers and taken me out to a nice dinner before the dance. I was really quite enamored with him despite his melancholy mood.

When we got to the dance both our spirits picked up quickly when I saw my friends and he could commiserate and scoff at the other team with his buddies. Soon we were dancing and the day's loss seemed history.

Driving home that night he started to kiss me, but I asked him to stop until he turned on the radio. Strangely enough, I was embarrassed to kiss without music. I don't know why. Maybe it was my way of diverting attention from myself and whatever inadequacies I felt at the time. It was also probably my way of adding a little more romance to the situation, somewhat lacking in a sky-blue Ford Maverick.

After several months of dating, we became close friends. Neither of us had been as intimate with anyone in our lives. We talked about school, our futures and what we would, or could not, achieve. We talked about our fears, our inadequacies and the general feelings of persecution all adolescents feel. Paul was petrified he wouldn't get into a decent college. He talked about it constantly. I, of course, had resigned myself not to think about it. I had miserable test scores and knew I would never get into any of the places my friends were going. We tried to talk each other out of these preconceptions of how are lives would turn. Sometimes it worked, sometimes it didn't. Nevertheless, it forced us to bond in a way I had never known with a member of the opposite sex. We grew and suffered together and, in turn, I began to love him. It was an all encompassing, dizzying effect new to me.

When we had first started going out, our dates weren't complicated. They consisted of going to a movie or party and then ending up at a parking lot near his house. We would make out for hours, and occasionally Paul would try things. I remember one time being caught by a police officer who was checking the grounds around the elementary school where we decided to "park." His flashlight caught the gleam of the buttons on my unbuttoned blouse. I didn't realize Paul had done this and was red with fury. Not only was I mortified by the policeman's approach but I had not given Paul permission for such a forward act. He apologized profusely and usually asked when he tried something new from then on.

Becoming sexually confident took some time. It also required a proclamation of love. I remember telling him I loved him very early on. I was somewhat hurt and disappointed when he didn't respond because it seemed like such a natural thing to say, but for him it was not. He later told me he wanted to say it then, but couldn't formulate the words. He didn't know why. It was months later when he whispered it quite hurriedly one night both because he meant it and because it was a ticket to more action. For me on the other hand, it was a prerequisite if anything more physical was to follow. I couldn't see sexually confiding in someone who didn't love me. I had enough trouble imagining what it would be like taking off my clothes in front of someone I did love. I didn't need, or want, to worry about whether or not he loved me back.

At sixteen, I thought it was very exciting to be dating a boy like Paul. He was on both the football and lacrosse teams, and I basked in the new attention associated with being his girlfriend. We went to dances, homecomings, proms, everywhere together. We had our share of fights as, for example, when he decided to vote for Homecoming Queen even after I had been dropped from the list, but we were basically having a lot of fun. We were such good friends and always laughed so much that whatever our problems, we tried to work them out. We would squabble about what would happen after we graduated, but that was usually short-lived.

After we had been dating for quite some time and had progressed quite comfortably to a particular point, we knew we were going to have sex sooner or later. We had taken our time and moved in stages from making out to heavy petting with or without clothes. It had taken me quite a long time to become comfortable with Paul and with my own body. I remember one time when he said in Spanish "I love your big breasts." I was so embarrassed I began to cry because "muchos globos" sounded so ugly. He tried to console me, saying it was a compliment, but I didn't believe him. It just made me feel different from everyone else, which horrified me. For at that age, to be different was not what I was striving for, yet I knew I was starting to become so.

Paul was very patient and gentle and never said "I think we should DO it." It was more of a silent agreement between the two of us. We had progressed to a stage where we would both be more physically satisfied if we did have sex. It was an urge mixed with curiosity and love, rather than just curiosity or urge alone.

One night we came home from a formal party and started making out. Portions of clothes were coming off and I said "No we can't, I . . . we don't have any birth control." Paul went sprinting upstairs and came back with this plastic package with a round ring inside. With a big grin on his face he said "Now we can." " No way" I said, "I am not losing my virginity on the floor of your living room."

Losing my virginity wasn't going to happen on a couch either. I refused to go that far without some kind of ambiance. I had been exposed to enough books and movies to know what kind of atmosphere I wanted. I wanted candles, violins, and no interruption. My dream scene did not include Johnny Carson's monologue.

When Paul came home after six weeks of camp counseling, we knew from our correspondence and from how anxious our bodies felt that we were ready for more than just making out. We planned the big moment when Paul's mother would be out of town. We had talked about it for weeks and concluded we wanted it to be special.

The night Paul's mother left, we watched television as usual. But after the ten o'clock show Paul scooped me up in his arms and carried me to his bedroom. I asked him why we didn't go to his mother's bed as it was bigger. He told me he felt that would be "sacrilegious to do the big it" in the room where his father had died. I didn't argue. So we went to Paul's second floor bedroom and he lay me down on the feather bed his grandfather had left him. It was a large, sumptuous bed with four oak posts which, in the dark, became phallic symbols in themselves. Paul was moving very slowly, and undressed me slowly with fluid motions as if he were taking petals off a flower. Once inside he moved even slower and asked me at every turn or twist of my face whether he was hurting me. Of course he was, but I just smiled and told him how happy I was to be there with him.

Now that I think back on it, actually I think the whole thing was very sweet. Neither one of us had any idea what to do or how we should feel. I was still somewhat shy about my body and insisted on keeping a pillow over my breasts until his chest was pressed up against mine.

The act itself was not physically fulfilling at all. It certainly didn't seem like the fireworks I had been promised on "Love American Style" reruns. In fact it was uncomfortable, somewhat painful and a shade strange. Fortunately, it was with someone I cared for deeply which made the whole thing worthwhile. I was becoming part of him and he of me. That was the important part.

Because Paul and I continued to date for several years we eventually got better at sex and enjoyed it more and more. Because of the stigma associated with having sex at that age, however, I often felt pangs of guilt about not waiting for marriage. I knew I loved Paul and he loved me, but we didn't really know what that meant. We thought we did, but who knows at such a young age? We knew we probably wouldn't stay together forever, so was this worth it? Such weighty matters often left me confused and worried. Strangely enough, these were the times I prayed very hard to God telling him I hoped I wasn't doing anything wrong. I would tell him I wasn't sure what I was doing, but that my intentions were good.

I didn't tell my closest friends I had had sex until months later. I was worried they would think me too promiscuous. In fact, I remember telling my closest friend, Charlotte, under some duress. We were having pizza one day, and in the middle of my sentence she asked, "Have you and Paul, you know?" I hesitated a little and sheepishly confessed we had. She looked at me quite seriously and then with a great sigh of relief said "Whew, so have Robert and I." I, too, was relieved.

Neither Paul nor I had ever talked about it with anyone but each other. It was such a relief, though, to talk with Charlotte who helped me realize there was nothing wrong with having sex as long as you cared about the person. She said the only time it felt really wrong was when you didn't know the person at all.

Paul and I went off to college. We gradually changed, developed new values, new priorities. I still had the hopes and dreams I shared with him years earlier, but now I was sharing them with new people. There is still a part of me that will always love Paul, not because he was a great lover or because I wish I could go back in time, but because of what we shared and what we meant to each other. Once you've experienced the combination of love and sex with someone, it never really goes away. It just settles somewhere else inside you until you inadvertently pull it out and remember it fondly.

As I have grown older, I have had sex without experiencing love, yet often with the hope love would follow. Sex without love is not, and never will be, fulfilling. Many women in college lived by the notion that "if it feels good, do it," and as a result had numerous lovers. This was before any of us knew AIDS would become so widespread in the heterosexual community.

Some of my friends and I have also had sex to overcome the loneliness or lack of warmth in our lives. Sometimes the sex is physically satisfying. Often, though, the emptiness which follows isn't eased by the sense of being the "Cosmopolitan" woman who can share a bed with different men and then claim victory. Some women try, of course, because men seem to find so much satisfaction in playing the field. Women feel they should be granted that same freedom without being judged adversely. But I don't know that I ever felt that freedom or that satisfaction with an anonymous lover. Of the experiences I have had, I cannot say that any were so physically stupendous as to supplant my wanting and needing to be loved.

20

AIDS and Early Sexual Experience

by J.D. Robinson, M.D.

AIDS will be part of our sexual and emotional landscape for the near and indefinite future. It is not about to go away. Quite the contrary, it is becoming a problem for more and more people who are younger and younger. In its simplest terms, AIDS is a uniformly fatal sexually transmitted disease which is also spread by blood. In a society used to making things come out our way, we have run up against something that cannot be fixed. Once you pick up AIDS you are stuck with it.

The human immunodeficiency virus, HIV, has been seeding the population in a major way for some fifteen years now. Mistaken notions have developed because the high risk behaviors engaged in by homosexuals and drug abusers have resulted in so many cases. These have overshadowed the somewhat less efficient spread by conventional heterosexual intercourse, which still has the capacity to produce a huge number of cases over time. The virus is now well outside groups engaging in the highest risk behaviors, intravenous needle sharing and receptive anal intercourse. At the same time, it is difficult to know who in particular is carrying the virus because it may cause apparently inconsequential symptoms for ten or more years before making its presence unavoidably obvious. For an individual, testing for the virus has some value. However, in a population frequently switching sexual partners its utility declines rapidly. As contacts multiply, a negative test rapidly becomes outdated information.

The Centers for Disease Control in Atlanta have now documented a quarter of a million cases of AIDS in the United States. Of this total, six percent are categorized as having been acquired heterosexually, which amounts to more than fifteen thousand people. Of cases reported in the past year, this has risen to nine percent, reflecting an increase in heterosexual transmission. More striking is that over the past year a full forty percent of cases in women have been acquired heterosexually. The CDC has accumulated almost fifty thousand cases from all causes in people in their twenties. Knowing what we do of the prolonged incubation period, most of these had to have been acquired during the teen-age years, which is to say, terribly early in the course of a person's life for a fatal disease.

Of what consequence is this knowledge for young people having their first sexual experience? The fact is that while HIV is difficult to transmit, it can under the right circumstances, be spread from one person to another with only one sexual contact. Estimates of the number of infected individuals in this country hover between a million and a million-and-a-half. Those carrying the virus are more likely to be males and members of minorities; however, HIV is by no means confined to these groups. While the transmission is more efficient from male to female, it can also be spread by female to male. Anal intercourse and intravenous injection remain the most efficient means of spread, but anyone who is already infected can pass the virus on by heterosexual activity; the method of acquiring the AIDS virus does not restrict the modes of spreading it. The virus is found in male sexual fluids, both the semen ejaculated from the penis and a small quantity which precedes the semen during male arousal. HIV is present in vaginal secretions and in any blood which might be in the vagina.

Passion is wet. When people have sex there is a lot of fluid about, male and female. By the time intercourse is completed these fluids are typically distributed, at the least, all over the sexual organs of both partners. If one of the individuals has the virus, there are ample opportunities to pass it to the other. This being said, not every such contact will result in transmission of the virus. The use of a condom can reduce, but not eliminate the risk, by covering the opening of the penis and by preventing the female from receiving an inoculation of male sexual fluid.

It is important to realize that a series of factors enhance the likelihood of transmission. Of great importance is the condition of the donor. As incubation proceeds over a number of years, the carrier of infection has an ever increasing load of virus particles, rendering the body fluids more infectious. The presence of any breaks in the skin or of any other venereal disease increases transmissibility. In addition, two anatomic factors play a role. Uncircumcised males are more likely to pick up the infection through the foreskin. Young girls in their first few years of menstruation typically have immature cells in the cervix, at the opening of the womb, which appear to be more vulnerable to infection.

It is a simple fact that for each couple, in each situation, there always seems to be a particular reason at hand why they can decide they are not at risk. That may be close to the truth in the majority of individual cases. Unfortunately, in the aggregate, such rationalizing adds up to a tremendous hazard. The persistence of a belief in invulnerability enhances that very vulnerability; the larger the number of people figuring they are not at risk, the greater the gamble for all of them. There is no easy answer to this dilemma. In the days when syphilis and gonorrhea carried a probability of causing disfigurement, derangement and death, there was still plenty of risky behavior and abundant transmission of these diseases. When the hazardous consequences of exceedingly pleasurable activity are far removed from that activity, few individuals are motivated to pause and contemplate the future. Recent studies continue to confirm that only a small segment of the population is taking AIDS seriously when making personal sexual decisions. By the turn of the century, an unfortunately large number of these people will be in for a very big surprise.

21

Choice

by Tilly Goldman

I remember every detail of the day I lost my virginity. It was my little sister's twelfth birthday and my parents were throwing a party for her. I was about sixteen, give or take a few months and dating a boy named Kevin. He lived in another town and didn't go to my high school, a very convenient set up. Kevin and a friend had decided to drive up for the afternoon and evening. He asked me to find a date for his friend so I invited Linda.

After playing with my sister's friends for awhile, we decided to take a walk in the park behind our house. This was not your ordinary park. It was hundreds of acres of beautifully manicured lawns and trees set on dramatically rolling hills overlooking miles of preserved farmland. I had spent much of my childhood in this park. It was there that I had learned to sled, ski, roll down hills and smoke cigarettes. It doesn't seem to surprise me that it was in this park that I had my biggest experience of growing up.

I can't remember whose suggestion it was to sit down, but before I knew it, Kevin and I were lying underneath a huge beech tree, and his friend and Linda were sitting next to each other about 50 yards away.

I remember asking him if he wanted to "do it" and his quick but stuttered reply, "yes." I was only briefly concerned about birth control and he quickly assured me he would pull out in time. I just wanted to do it and finish. I hardly felt anything at all. I remember being pushed back and forth, moving under him and listening to him grunt. It didn't really hurt that much. Lying on top of the tree roots hurt more.

The whole thing took about ten minutes, if that, and when he was finished, he very thoughtfully came on my skirt. The most intense aspect of the whole experience was a tremendous thunder and lightning storm that arose and made things a bit more climactic.

We quickly dressed and started back to the house. At this point, the only emotions going through my head were those of regret and disappointment. I wasn't feeling the incredible satisfaction and pleasure I thought I would. In a way, I wanted to run home to my mother, tell her everything and hear her assure me that everything was going to be fine. I didn't even want to talk to Kevin; I just wanted him to leave. Sex was not what it was supposed to be.

Of course, my parents had suspected nothing. I spent the rest of the night telling my friend Linda all the dirty details. She seemed interested in what I had to say, but I could tell she wasn't planning on giving her virginity up as apathetically and I admired her for that.

The next day at school, the news spread quickly among my girlfriends. Their reactions were all different—some negative, some positive, but they all had opinions. I guess it was because I was the first to do it.

As the school year drew to a close, Kevin and I saw less and less of each other. He was planning on spending the summer at home working in a gas station, and I was planning on working at the beach and living with Linda and another girl for the summer. Of course, I promised we would keep in touch and reassured him that he could come down anytime and visit.

Although we telephoned each other for the first few weeks, I felt myself enjoying our conversations less and less and wanting to meet other boys more and more. I did eventually meet another guy whose house was right down the street, so we started seeing a lot of each other. I think Kevin knew at this point that there was someone else.

The amount of his desperation at the thought of losing me came to a head during one of our nightly conversations. He accused me of being distant and unresponsive and we started to fight. I ended the call by hanging up on him. I was relieved that I didn't have to talk to him anymore that night and quickly ran out of the house so I didn't have to answer the phone.

Later that night, I was sitting on the front porch with my new boyfriend when Kevin drove up. Unfortunately, I was kissing the guy at the time. I ran into the house, locked myself in the bathroom and sat there petrified of what he would do. Luckily, all that happened was some name-calling and some huffing and puffing. I remember feeling incredibly guilty after he left, but also feeling even more relieved that it was over. The sad part about the whole situation was that he had driven 200 miles just to say he was sorry for our fight over the phone.

As the end of July approached, it was time to quit my job and come home. Our family always spends the month of August in Maine. I had had a great time experimenting with my new independence but couldn't wait to get home to the cleanliness and security of my own home.

Coming home also meant facing the fact that I hadn't gotten my period in over a month. After a week, I decided to get tested at the local women's center. Luckily my friend Pam was around and offered to drive me down. Getting tested was a lot easier than I thought. All you had to do was pee in a jar and bring it in. The hard part was waiting the next three hours to hear the results.

Pam and I just sat in my room and stared at each other until it was time to call. I couldn't bring myself to pick up the phone, so she very thoughtfully offered to call. I heard her hang up and slowly walk back into my room "Well?" I said. She nodded her head and looked slowly down at the floor. I can't remember how long I cried. All I know is that I couldn't believe it was happening to me. I had only had sex once. No one gets pregnant after her first time.

Pam finally got me somewhat together and told me it was time to make a decision. I knew that too, but was too afraid of the choices. After a lot of talk, we decided the only thing to do was to get an abortion. She knew of a place and immediately called for an appointment for me.

The next decision was whether or not I should call Kevin. Unfortunately, I had absolutely no money and knew I couldn't go to my parents. The only solution was to call. Of course, I didn't have the guts after what happened at the beach, so Pam again helped me out.

I listened to her side of the conversation and couldn't believe when I heard "Of course it's yours. . . ." I guess he had every right to ask after seeing me with that other guy. Even so, I was a bit hurt by the remark. He eventually agreed to put up half the money which, at the time, was $ 75. The next question was where I would get the other $ 75. Once again, Pam pulled through by offering a loan.

The appointment was the following morning so I had to come up with a quick excuse. I told my parents that Pam and I were going to an amusement park and that I had to get up very early. I slept fine that night probably because I had no idea what the next day held for me.

The actual procedure took all day due to the five hours of counseling they put you through before going up on the table. I don't remember much about the day except the scene inside the operating room (if that's what it's called). I remember a bucket on the floor half filled with what I thought were aborted fetuses. There was some blood on the floor and in the sink. Luckily, they had given me some valium so I wasn't too grossed out.

We were put in a group recovery room for about an hour and given juice and cookies to help regain our strength. I couldn't believe the variety of women there. They were all ages and races. I guess unwanted pregnancies have no limits.

Pam picked me up and drove me to her house so I could sleep off the pain a little. When I eventually got home, no one could tell that anything had gone on, and I assured Mom that we had had a great day.

I probably would have kept the whole thing a secret if I hadn't had to figure out some way to pay Pam back. I knew I had to confide in my mother; she would be the only one who could help.

I decided to tell her after dinner one night in Maine. I had had a hard enough time explaining why I couldn't play tennis, let alone not swim. She was speechless at first, but soon came around and asked how it had happened and with whom. I hated telling her, but felt incredibly relieved afterwards. It was as though I had cleansed my soul and come to terms with my uncomfortable feeling about what I had done. Of course, she offered to lend me the money to pay Pam provided I work around the house to pay her back.

I made her swear she wouldn't tell anybody especially my father. I could never look him in the eye again if he found out. I knew he would understand and support me, but I didn't want to disappoint him. I'm sure Mom told him eventually. She's the type of person who needs to share everything with her husband.

That summer held the best and the worst times of my life. On the one hand, I had found a newly independent side of my personality while spending time at the beach. On the other, I had lost the only untouched part of my childhood and with unpleasant results. I will never forget the incredible support from my mother and Pam. Pam and I are still friends and we see each other often, but never mention our experience.

I have slept with several men since then and have thought of this experience every time. I was probably being taught a lesson when I got pregnant; I'm not entirely sure what the lesson was. I do know it was wrong to rush into it and to want to do it just for the sake of doing it. Although I enjoyed the thrill and was proud of the accomplishment at the time, the experience will always remain in my mind as an uncomfortable one, one I wish I could erase. My sadness is not because I "did it" but because I was so anxious to try it and know I'd done it. Most of my friends have smiles on their faces when they talk about their first time. Whenever I think about mine, I want to cry.

22

Virgin

by Sarah Hardin

I am nineteen and a virgin. Yes, I feel as though I am in a support group confessing a strange and unaccepted problem, but unfortunately there are no support groups for virgins, probably because there are so few in our society today. I am not some sort of freak or religious fanatic. I am very average in many ways, except that I am a virgin. This seems to set me apart.

Many guys find me attractive both mentally and physically. I have no problem finding dates, that is until word gets around that I don't "put out." Peoples' responses to my virginity vary. Usually they try to come up with an excuse for why I haven't had intercourse. Some people assume I have been raped or molested, while others ask if anyone has asked me to have sex, assuming that I wanted to, but was a nice girl who didn't want to make the first move. None of these reasons explains why I choose to be a virgin, and yes, it is my choice.

I pride myself on being a very independent person who makes rational decisions in my life. Part of the decision-making process is knowing what I am comfortable with and what choices could lead to regret. Therefore, I usually put off making decisions until I am absolutely sure I am happy with the reasons I am making the decision, and have thought of all the consequences and have decided I will have no regrets. This is part of the reason I have chosen to be a virgin.

Being a virgin is one thing in my life I have almost complete control over, short of being raped. My virginity is the one thing I can choose when, where, and to whom I shall give it. My virginity is a gift that I am saving for my future husband. It is the single most important gift I can give to the man with whom I choose to spend the rest of my life, and it wouldn't be fair to either him or me to give it away to someone who is not worthy of it.

I want to make love the first time I have intercourse. For too many women their first time is just a sexual experience with someone they don't know. But just being in love isn't enough to me. The man I give my virginity to will love me for everything just as I am. We will have a bond of trust so strong beforehand that making love will be a natural act for us and not an act that will strain our relationship.

Intercourse is such an intimate thing that it often creates problems of confusion and misunderstanding. If the relationship is strong before sex, it can endure the more complicated problems afterward.

When I first started dating Bo, I felt the pressure of the sex issue in the back of my head haunting me every moment until I decided our relationship could not progress until I told him my feelings. This was very difficult for me to do. At first, I asked Bo if we could just be friends and get to know each other slowly, but after talking for awhile, I told him that I didn't just want to be friends, but that our relationship would not progress to the point of having sex. Even though I thought our relationship could possibly grow to a point where I would feel comfortable enough to make love with him, I didn't want him to wonder when the time would come that I would love him enough to give him my virginity. I wanted him to stay with me knowing he could never take my virginity away.

When I first told Bo there would be no sex, he said, "That's okay; I am not driven by sex; I don't need to have it." He laughed at me for worrying so much about it. He told me that the reason he wanted to get to know me was not in order to have sex with me. This made me feel better, and I could relax knowing that he wouldn't just walk away like some guys would.

I knew this would be a change of pace for Bo since he is twenty-eight and has had sex before in two previous relationships. He recently said to me in one of our many talks spent trying to make our relationship work, "I've never had a girl that hasn't wanted to have sex with me; some have even given me their virginity." I can see why. Bo is a very good-looking, well-respected man. It is almost impossible to get him to notice you.

The first time I spent the night at his apartment, he promised he wouldn't try anything, and he didn't. He did warn me, however, that if people found out, they would assume we had had sex. That bothered me. My sex life is nobody's business unless I choose it to be. I hated the thought that people would gossip about me. As I walked back to my room the next morning someone shouted across the lawn, "Did you get a piece?" I was enraged and embarrassed. Why can't two people spend the night together and just sleep and talk? Why is it that they are expected to have sex?

Our relationship progressed, and things seemed to be going fine until one night when Bo came to my room and told me we only had two months left before we would go our separate ways during the summer. Instead of treasuring the time we had left, he was adamant that we break up at that moment and save ourselves the pain it would cause later. He asked me what I wanted and I told him I wanted to stay together. As he saw tears come to my eyes, he said, "Okay, we can stay together; I've changed my mind." I knew then and there that he wasn't telling me the whole story. He later told me he had been having sexual dreams about me and thought I would be upset if I knew. I wasn't upset and encouraged him to share everything with me.

We continued to learn about each other and our relationship grew stronger, but he soon started making little comments to me about sex which greatly upset me. I remember distinctly one night after he sang the national anthem in front of the crowd at a basketball play-off game, he called me from a party and asked if he had done okay. I enthusiastically said how wonderful he had sounded. He responded by asking if it made me want to have sex with him since a lot of other girls had come up to him afterward and told him his singing had really turned them on. They had given him their phone numbers in case he ever wanted to take them up on their offers of sex, no strings attached, just sex and then never talk again.

I told him to take the offers if that was what he wanted. After apologizing profusely, he told me it had just been on his mind a lot lately. The rest of the week we talked on the phone every night, but he could never find the time to see me. I thought this was strange since I knew he hated talking on the phone, but I let it go. Toward the end of the week I finally asked why he was avoiding seeing me. He confessed that he now just couldn't handle being intimate without having sex even though he had told me otherwise at the beginning of our relationship. He proposed that we spend time together and just be friends. I went along with it, but knew from previous experience that when two people care about each other as more than just friends, it is impossible to pretend that sexual feelings don't exist.

The next time we were together, it was just like it had always been except there was a boundary at first with touching. He continued to tell me how beautiful he thought I was and how much he liked me, and I continued to play along, like friends, ignoring his comments. When he began to fall asleep, I jumped up and announced I was leaving and that

I'd see him the next day. He started whining, asking me to spend the night with him, as friends, "just like a slumber party." I wanted to spend the night and did. We went to bed on opposite sides with no touching involved and fell right to sleep. About three hours later I woke up to his restlessness and asked why he couldn't sleep. He told me the reason was that I hadn't spent the night in so long and he just wanted to reach over and hold me. This got us talking about our relationship. I asked him if he wanted to give it another try and he did. Even though I felt uncomfortable, I told him I would perform oral sex on him. I guess I felt like it would be an apology for not having sex. He knew I was uncomfortable and told me it would be all right if I didn't want to do it. I respected and thanked him for not taking advantage of my offer.

Our relationship seemed to hit a wall. As Bo put it, we just had two different viewpoints on the relationship. At first it had been fine not to have sex, but then he really started to like me and didn't want to hold anything back. He wanted to continue to grow closer to me by making love. I corrected him by saying it would just be sex between us because although we cared about each other, we did not love each other.

I told him that if I did have sex with him, it would ruin our relationship for several reasons. First, I would be having sex to save a relationship that wouldn't last anyway if he wasn't willing to stay in it without sex. Secondly, I would become too emotionally attached to him. By sharing something so intimate, I was afraid my feelings would become more sensitive and hurt much more easily, fearing and doubting that he didn't care for me as much as I did for him. This fear was rooted in the fact that I would be giving up something for him I could never get back, while he would be giving up nothing. The last reason came from the knowledge that sex would mean more to me than it would him, therefore putting me in a position where he had control over my actions and emotions. He felt it was unfair of me to assume that sex wouldn't mean as much to him.

One time when we were fooling around I thought for a brief moment that sex wouldn't be that big a deal, since we had been going through the motions all the time anyway. I feel so fortunate that thought stopped there and never entered my mind again. After hearing all my friends' stories about how they lost their virginity and how they wished they were in my position again, I wonder if I ever want to risk getting hurt by having sex before marriage.

I care about Bo and am thankful he has always been honest with me about his feelings. He tells me he cares about me, but he just needs to find a relationship that is "half as terrific" as ours but with someone he can have sex with. He says he just wasn't as strong as he thought, but I look at it as if his feelings for me were not as strong as I thought. Sex is the ultimate test to see how much a guy really cares for a girl mentally, because if his mental love is strong enough, he will give up the physical part just to have a girl mentally. I do think Bo's intentions were good, but for him he needed to have the physical part to make the mental part better. For I know that I need to find a man who will love me so much mentally that he would wait for me forever physically.

I have given up trying to make things work with Bo. I realize his feelings for me aren't as strong as I need them to be, and that time will make them even weaker if he is struggling now. I guess we were just meant to be friends, and I know one day I will find someone who will wait for me physically because he loves me mentally. While I am waiting, I am content to know that the decisions I make are for my happiness.

Before I got into my relationship with Bo, I figured I would have sex with the first guy I truly loved and trusted, but now I have decided I want to wait until marriage. If sex is so great, why is it that every time a woman finds out I am a virgin I gain a whole new respect in her eyes and she tells me how she wishes she were a virgin again. And why is it that some women can't even talk about how they lost their virginity without breaking into tears, even if it happened five years earlier. The pain and emotion that go into sharing yourself for the first time are a big deal. It is too bad that too many girls get rushed and pressured into having sex before they are ready or for the wrong reasons. Sex is a personal thing and should be only shared with a person that can be trusted with your darkest secrets, but for so many girls and women it is used in place of attention, excitement, and love. I believe you can have all of these things and sex too. Good things come to those who wait, and that is why I am waiting.

Bo has most recently decided that we can be nothing more than friends. His reason is out of respect for me. He feels that if we stay together as more than friends, he will ask me to have sex with him. He knows this would hurt me and destroy most of the trust he has worked so hard to earn from me. He says he wants me to remember him as a man I respect and who respected me. He wants me to remember him as someone good, not bad, in my life. I will always remember the good times with him, but I will also remember that the last three weeks of our relationship centered around sex issues.

Some people seem to think it was our nine year age difference that finally split us apart. "It's a difference in life styles," they would say, but age was never an issue. Our relationship endured other difficult barriers as well such as being a racially mixed couple, but our relationship was never strong enough to keep us together without sex. Sex is the ultimate test of a relationship, but I abstain for the personal reasons I have stated. What would your mate do if you suddenly told him you weren't comfortable having sex with him any more. Would he stick by your side? Maybe you should try it. For me it is better to find out earlier rather than later once I am so attached that it would absolutely break my heart to find out he doesn't care as much as I thought. This is why I am dealing well with my breakup with Bo. I realize that although he is a wonderful person, he is not what I am looking for, and I don't like to settle for anything less than the best!

23

Date Rape

by Patricia Sole

Reminiscing on how I lost my virginity, several pictures flash through my mind. I had one very bad experience and one very good experience. The way sex was treated in my family and among my peers greatly shaped my sexual behavior and feelings about virginity and women's sexuality.

I grew up in a small, white, middle class suburb of a mid-size Ohio city, and my parents were fairly religious. My mother in particular exhibited that unmistakable Protestant sexual uptightness. When I talk about my mom's sexual uptightness, I think that it was a reflection of both society and her religious background. She epitomized the traditional feminine role of wife, mother and caretaker. She always said she did not want to work outside the home. I think my father liked that idea, kind of a deal they made when they were courting. My father frequently traveled so my mom really had the brunt of the caretaking of my sister and me.

Sex was rarely discussed openly in our house. I think it was embarrassing for my mom to talk about stuff like this with us. Instead it was alluded to in terms of what was socially acceptable behavior. For example, I remember when I had my first period, my mom told me to ask my sister how to use tampons because she did not use them. My sister didn't want to show me either, so I learned from a friend. The point is that we did not openly discuss this new aspect of my femininity and sexuality. Instead, I was left to figure it out on my own.

When we were small, my mom sat down and honestly explained the whole "how babies are made" story. It wasn't the reproductive part of sex she had problems with, but the "sex" and "intimacy" part. Birth control was never discussed because it was implicit we would not have sex outside marriage so therefore we did not need to discuss it. I never discussed sexual intimacy with my parents, or how pleasurable sex could be, or birth control. I never really formed my own opinion about these issues until I went away to college.

My mother told us outright that sex outside marriage could only lead to trouble for a variety of reasons. An impeccable family and personal reputation was a high priority to my parents, and this carried over into what I thought of myself and my reputation in our community. Unwanted pregnancy looked bad. Illegitimate children could negatively affect my sister and me for the rest of our lives.

Abortion wasn't discussed either. I don't think it was even viewed as an option by my parents, but it was by me. I thought abortion was certainly better than being completely shamed and humiliated by having an illegitimate child. Marrying the boy would be completely out of the question; who would want to ruin her life being married with a baby at 16 or 17? I recall thinking how mentally wrenching an abortion must be—but well worth the personal trauma. I did not believe, then or now, that it was murder, killing a child. That has never been an issue for me. It is the woman's choice whether or not she wants to carry a group of cells to term to be a living human being.

My parents had instilled in us the idea that we could do or be whatever we wanted, doctors, lawyers or teachers. There was no question that our future encompassed going to college and myriad other options such as starting a career or continuing on to graduate school. A family would come later in life, along with the requisite husband, house, car and two-week vacation. We would have the dream of full-time motherhood to look forward to at that juncture in our lives. In spite of all this, the real message we got was that, really, the most important thing a woman could do with her life was to become a wife and mother. These were the values of my parents, my church and our community.

At home I learned there were three major sexual taboos. First, it was immoral for either a man or woman to have sex outside the confines of marriage because it went against our religious teachings and practices. We were raised with the ideal of the sanctity of marriage. Second, men often just wanted sex from women so we needed to beware—you could not always trust men. Once they were getting sex they lost respect for you. Respect was always a big issue for my mother. If you were having sex with a man, why would he bother to marry you? She often referred to the phrase "Why buy the cow when you can get the milk free?" I think this was a common enough philosophy for mothers to hand down to their daughters. My mom wanted to protect us; she did not want us to be hurt. For her the progression of male-female relationships was to date, find a man you loved, get married, then have sex. Sex seemed to be fine within the confines of marriage; it wasn't dirty or bad or anything like that, but it was not right outside of marriage. Finally, there was the risk of unwanted pregnancy, a fear that only women are burdened with. A man can just walk away from this situation. You can't force a man to marry you or help raise your child.

My family's approach to sex education seemed to differ from the traditional moral upbringing of my Catholic girlfriends. Not only did they openly discuss sex with their parents, the idea that sex and abortion were "sinful" was ingrained into their heads at an early age. I always thought it ironic that my Catholic girlfriends both in high school and college chose to have abortions rather than carry the child to term and give it up for adoption.

Regardless of one's religious background, the double standard that men played around and women remained pure and virtuous was a constant. This was acknowledged by all women, and adopting a casual attitude about sex was definitely not what a good girl did.

I think it is also important to remember that there are two parts of sex, mental and physical. I have talked a lot about how family and community values figure into the mental aspect of sex. Now I want to focus on the physical aspects which I learned from my peers.

In high school I had boyfriends and fooled around but I remember it wasn't always particularly pleasant, and sometimes these sexual explorations were downright painful! Sometimes I did stuff because I was interested in exploring sex, and sometimes because I thought that the boy would not like me anymore if I didn't do stuff with him. This is painful for me to acknowledge, but I think it is common to male-female relationships particularly in the teen years. Because of certain societal values, women are given two opposite messages: men want to have sex with women, but women who are sexually active are not respected. There is no easy answer to this dilemma. But girls need to face it and discuss it with their friends and parents/counselors.

A young woman often is not as easily gratified as a young man. It is her responsibility to learn about her body by herself or with a caring partner so she can know what she likes and what makes her feel good. She does this by learning about her physical anatomy and by touching and feeling herself. This is a normal and healthy exploration process and should be encouraged.

Because I was never seriously in love in high school, I never really experienced a lot of pressure from anyone to have sex and remained a virgin throughout high school. Many of my friends had serious relationships at this time and experienced sex at age 16 or 17. Unfortunately, many of them had unpleasant experiences and at least half ended up having abortions. They either did not use birth control or they and their partners did not understand it. We may have had similar parental experiences: birth control wasn't talked about because parents did not want to seem as if they were condoning premarital sex. Many of these girls underwent abortions without the support of their parents because they were too frightened to confide in them. Often their boyfriends were just as scared and reacted to the situation by dumping them. So they were left to deal with the problem by themselves and felt even more scared, alone and ashamed.

Seeing these incidents was much more of a deterrent from sex than any caution from my parents. Watching my friends go through this terribly difficult situation, I gained a real fear of pregnancy. As a result, I am against "pressured" or "spur-of-the-moment" sex. Young women need to know what they are getting into when they engage in sex, and they need to understand birth control. The benefits often do not outweigh the risks, particularly for females.

I was seventeen when I first entered college. That fall semester, I was the victim of date rape by an older student at the university. I never told anyone about this experience until several years later. I think that even now I do not understand the complete ramifications of this incident on my psyche.

It happened like this. I was out in a bar with a group of my girlfriends. I started talking to a hockey player and we went to another bar together. We were both drinking heavily. After the bars closed, we went back to his apartment to cook breakfast. This might sound strange, but it was a common occurrence among my friends that we would often party until early morning and either go out to breakfast or back to a friend's apartment to eat together. I started cooking and he said he had to go to the bathroom and left the kitchen. I resumed cooking—we were making Kraft macaroni and cheese—with my back to him.

When he came back from the bathroom, he was naked. He put his arms around me from behind and started touching me and trying to kiss me. I remember thinking—this guy is crazy, I have to get out of here. I tried to laugh off his behavior by telling him to stop. I was hungry and wanted to eat the breakfast that I was cooking. The rest is blurry—but I remember I was on the floor of the living room next to the kitchen and he was on top of me and would not stop touching me. I did not want to be there with him on top of me—but he forced me, physically holding me down. He was hurting me trying to force himself inside me—I had never been penetrated before and I was terrified. He couldn't penetrate me because I was so dry, so he dragged me with him into the kitchen and got a stick of butter, used that to lubricate me and forced himself in me. I was crying and telling him to stop, that it hurt, that I didn't want to, that I was only seventeen and please to stop it, but he ignored me. I remember feeling his weight on me and feeling powerless because I physically could not stop him.

Afterwards he acted like nothing had happened. I was still crying and he got dressed and drove me home. When we pulled in the parking lot of my dorm, he turned to me and said "You're only seventeen? I'm sorry." I looked at him and said, "Why are you sorry, do you have a sister who is seventeen? Would you like her treated this way?" He said, "Yeah, I do have a sister your age." It was only in retrospect that I think he was questioning me because at seventeen I was still a minor and it could have been statutory rape. I think that was his only concern.

I remember getting back to the warmth and safety of my dorm room where everything was as I had left it the night before. There was amazing succor in the knowledge that I was safe there, that at least nothing had changed in my little room. I stared at my face in the mirror covered with mascara where my tears had smeared my make-up. Sadly, it never occurred to me to file charges or even to accuse him of rape. At that time I had never heard of date rape and just assumed that the whole incident was my fault. I was so ashamed I couldn't discuss the incident with anyone. I never got counseling or even talked about it until at least 3–4 years later.

What should a young woman do when this happens? She should report it, get counseling and stop blaming herself. Most important, she should make sure she understands what kind of situation she may be getting into. When I went to college I was so naive, it never occurred to me people behaved in that manner. I did not know people hurt other people deliberately. I later learned this same man sexually abused another young woman on campus. He was obviously a repeat abuser, but even that knowledge did not stop me from blaming myself about the incident. I am now 28 and realize his behavior was totally unacceptable.

After that, the major sexual issue for me was that of trust and safety, not love. I still considered myself to be a virgin, because that violent sexual act had not been of my own free will. My virginity was still mine, something secure, to keep for myself or to give away to someone else by conscious decision. It would have been a defeat to the rapist to think that something that much my own could be taken away in a few minutes.

I had not confided in anyone about the rape and simply blocked it from my memory for several years and continued dating and seeing men. My sexual explorations continued but I was what is called "a tease." I would mess around but never have actual intercourse. I was never abused by anyone else either. As the only self-acknowledged virgin among my friends in college, I was the object of much teasing. I participated in the gossip about sex and men as much as the next woman, and took the teasing about my virginity in a good-natured fashion. Some of my friends even said they wished they had waited until they were older to have sex as it would have been more meaningful to them.

As a four-year member of a sorority, the Saturday morning hash session was *de rigueur* in my house. In hilarious, excruciating detail, all aspects of men and sex were discussed at length—how big a particular guy's penis was, whether he liked to have oral sex—did we give him a blow job—did we have an orgasm? Was he a talker in bed or was he quiet during sex? To this day, even if I don't see a sorority sister for a couple of years—I can sit down with her and talk about sex without any embarrassment. It is a close, nice feeling—the feeling you have when you can share secrets with someone.

As college progressed, my ideas about sex changed a lot. No longer under the influence of my parents, I was experimenting with my first real taste of freedom. A lot of people seemed to be having casual sex, and I felt as if perhaps it wasn't that immoral after all. For the first time sex became something you did because it felt good—it was pleasurable. College opened my eyes in this respect. But there was still that "good girl" stereotype that I carried around with me that also permeated the campus—the idea that "good girls" don't sleep around. If you slept around, men would only like you for sex not for a dating relationship. Dating relationships were encouraged not only because it was wonderful to be in love but because they led to marriage. As I said, in my traditional upbringing, marriage was the natural end to a relationship. It was like this: "Good girls" had steady boyfriends, got pinned to a fraternity boy, got engaged and then got the big prize—Marriage. "Bad girls", the "sleep-around" kind, might never catch a man, might never get married.

I was twenty the spring of my junior year in college when I went home for the weekend to visit my parents and met a much older man, seventeen years older. We started a long distance friendship as my university was about two hours from the city in which he lived. That summer, we saw each other almost every day, but I had to sneak because, of course, my parents disapproved of the relationship. Weeks went by and we messed around, but I still abstained from intercourse, much to his consternation and growing frustration. I think I relished this modicum of control, and obviously was still dealing with the rape experience. Unconsciously I think, it seemed that if I had sex I would be losing control of myself and that was one of the reasons I had never had intercourse.

One weekend I was invited to an out-of-town wedding, and my guy and I were in a fight. I ended up going alone, but after a few cocktails called him and invited him to come down to the reception late and spend the night. He arrived and we enjoyed ourselves, then went to a bar with the rest of the wedding party.

Finally it was time to find a hotel room. At this point, I knew I was actually going to do it. We had discussed having sex together before several times and now I was ready to give it a try. I did not love him at this point in the relationship, but to be frank, I wanted to see what it would be like.

We rented a room at the Dayton Sheraton. It was very late and obviously we had both been drinking. The night clerk must have wanted to play a trick on us. She gave us our key and when we opened the door, we found an enormous suite with a huge bed, red wallpaper and mirrored walls surrounding the bed and covering the ceiling! The floor had red plush carpet on it. Three steps led up to the bed as if it were some type of sacrificial alter. I felt as if I were in a New Orleans bordello, the kind you see on TV in 19th century period movies! I do not know how else to get the point across, but this was not an ordinary hotel room in Dayton, Ohio!

I remember thinking, I hope it doesn't hurt. That was my main concern, not getting pregnant or being immoral. I wanted him to enjoy it and like having sex with me, but my main concern this first time was myself and my own needs. I didn't need to worry about whether he would still like me in the morning. I had built a relationship with this person and trusted him and felt safe. This knowledge overcame my prior scary and horrible memories of intimacy.

It did not hurt, and I distinctly remember waking up the next morning and seeing us in the mirror above the bed. I felt great because it was over and had been very pleasant, not scary or uncomfortable at all. I was initiated into sex with someone who was able to teach me to respect my body and who cared about me. Through this positive experience I learned how to feel good about sex and to enjoy it.

The message I want to convey to young women and parents/counselors is that all aspects of sex must be thought through and discussed at great length. Young women need to understand the full ramifications of their sexual behavior. Pregnancy and date rape can happen to anyone. Young women need to be educated about these issues as well as about birth control. You do not need to be a victim. If you are abused, it is possible to overcome it with counseling and a caring, understanding partner. There is no need to be ashamed.

Second, when I was in high school and college, there was no AIDS epidemic to contend with in the midwest, so that risk did not affect my feelings about sex or my sexual behavior. That is no longer the case, and AIDS must figure heavily into *every* conversation about sexual activity.

I hope all young women begin their sexual experiences with a loving, trusting partner. I know this is often not the case, particularly as society pressures young people to grow up so quickly. It is most important to feel right about the decision to have sex, whether it is the first time or not. Sex will not be enjoyable unless you feel good about yourself and the person you are with. Women can take control of their sexual actions in a positive, responsible way. We can choose when and with whom to have our first sexual encounter.

24

Communicating Sexuality: How You Talk About Sex May Be More Important Than What You Say

by Caryl T. Moy, MSW, Ph.D.

"Want to go to bed?"
"Let's do it."
"You would if you loved me!"
"What would you think of spending the night with me?"
"I want to make love to you."

These are just a few lines a person might use, hoping to have sex with you. You may have spoken similar words yourself. Of the examples given, which one feels most caring? Most demanding? Do any comments you've experienced seem demeaning or threatening? Do any "celebrate" you, make you feel truly unique or special? Do any acknowledge your feelings—your eagerness or worry about first-time intercourse? The intention of each of these invitations can produce a different response.

If we analyze the concept of sexual communication, we see a process in which individuals come to know and understand one another through voice, words, gestures, movements and touch. Ideas, facts, attitudes and emotions are active ingredients of a relationship with the result that strangers become friends, friends become lovers, and lovers occasionally revert to friends. The fundamental aspect of this communication is that it permits people to enter into intimate relationships and communicate their sexuality.

Before talking *about* sexuality, we should look at how people talk about sexuality. From the time we are young children, we are taught in various ways not to talk about sex. We are hushed and shushed. If we don't get a reprimand for asking, "What does it feel like to have sex?" we get a frown, a distraction or no answer at all. Parents, teachers, ministers and doctors are all too likely to convey the same message. Few adults feel comfortable letting their child know that sex can provide a special, fulfilling pleasure. They are apt to feel more at ease giving impersonal, scientific data about sperm and ovum or hazy, negative moralistic threats. This sexual taboo by the adult world as youth enters puberty has a cyclical effect which frequently results in our own reticence to talk frankly about sex. This socially reinforced attitude erects barriers separating people from one another and suppressing feelings of tenderness and normal sexual urges.

Another factor in talking about sex is the appropriate vocabulary to use. Scientific words seem stuffy; graphic words vulgar, obscene or aggressive. Few convey a sense of personal involvement. "To copulate" is scientifically detached. "To fuck" is void of the feeling one might want to share with a lover. "Sexual intercourse" may be more comfortable, but awkward. "Making love" comes closest to the desired feeling and involvement, but may not work for everyone.

The combination of historically repressed sexual communication and difficult choice of language results in hard to initiate verbal communication. The difficulty can be reduced by first discussing how one feels about talking about sexuality.

* * *

"I feel nervous, scared."
"I'd rather discuss it some other time, somewhere else."
"I'm wondering why you want to talk about it."
"What's the big deal?"

These expressions of feelings about sexual communication can clear the path for less inhibited discussion. However, an environment of acceptance and trust must be established between two people for sexual communication to be productive in enriching the relationship. Challenging or negative statements such as, "You shouldn't feel that way!" "That's just silly," or "Oh come on, why?" immediately trigger a defensive response which can weaken the connection.

How much more inviting and affirmative is a strong acceptance like, "It's a relief to get it out in the open, isn't it?" This principle of talking about *talking about* a subject can apply equally in all relationships—parent/child, teacher/student, physician/patient, as well as to the most intimate of interpersonal situations with a loving partner.

Many textbooks or paperbacks on relationships stress the importance of communication in establishing and maintaining relationships that provide the special satisfying qualities. Only recently has there been a developing awareness of ways to learn specific techniques to consciously make changes in interpersonal communication, and in sexual communication in particular.

Types of Communication

It can be helpful to think of verbal communication in terms of four basic styles, each with its own intentions and behaviors. Style One is used when information is simply being exchanged. It is usually friendly, sociable and tension-free. Examples of this style are:
"The semester is over and I can relax."
"I still long for a cigarette."
"Are you ready to eat?"

This style transfers to "want to go to bed" style sexual communication as follows:
"It was fun in bed last night."
"I'm going to take a shower before we make love."
"Should I light some candles?"

Style II is used when one wants to be persuasive or control a situation. It usually has the intention of forcing change in another person. A light Style II is a comfortable style, such as in selling, advocating or lecturing. "Let's do it," is a good example. But in dealing with relationship issues, a heavy Style II frequently involves high risk which can result in weakening the connection between two people.
"If you'd only listen."
"Do as I say."
"You don't know what you're talking about."

When sexual disagreements occur, often Style II manifests itself as follows:
"You should have come by now!"
"You only think of yourself."
"You never seem excited about sex."

The voice is often loud, authoritative, with a sarcastic tone, or perhaps deceptively soft, seductive or whiny. "You would if you loved me," is a Style II statement.

For persons building good sexual communication, Style III, with its tentative and speculative tone provides a comfortable way to talk about sex.

"What would happen if we made love in the living room?"

"I'm wondering if we could get together this evening when both of us are done working."

"What would you think of making love in the morning?"

There may be a little hesitancy, but the voice is calm and quiet. In this style the speaker speaks for her/himself. It is useful in dealing with issues, but limited because feelings are expressed tentatively or not at all.

Style IV is natural for good sexual communication. It provides for mutuality, for each partner to be the authority for his/her own sexual satisfaction. It is committed, the intention to allow each partner to work for the common cause. It is "heavy," a mode that one probably does not want to be in too many times during the day. In Style IV, each partner wants to be open and direct. Each tunes into his/her own self-awareness, translating it into words and sharing it with the partner. The intention is full and honest disclosure. This also allows for the understanding of the partner's self-awareness. The most important intention is the caring and mutual support of both partners for themselves and each other.

"You know, when we go over a week without making love, I get scared that you really don't want to make love with me or that maybe you want it with somebody else."

"I really want to be with you, but I don't know how to tell you, and I don't get any message that you want to make love with me."

"It's such a special feeling that I have when I'm around you. I want to shut out the other parts of my life and just focus on you and your needs. It's a feeling I've never had before, and I wanted to tell you that."

"I have a hard time telling you this because I know it upsets you so."

In this style, voice quality is usually calm and caring; body language is congruent with intention. "I want to make love to you," is a good starting Style IV statement.

Styles III and IV allow for the most effective communication about sexuality as they are high in receptivity and self-disclosure respectively. Sharing a sexual experience with a partner is the most intimate kind of communication. When caring, trusting, autonomous verbal communication is used to enhance the total experience, it is bonding for both partners and increases the intimacy between them. Understanding how one talks can make a difference in that communication.

25

Patience is a Virtue

by M. Hunter Marks

Jackie and I were together four days short of a year before we made love for the first time. I wanted to be as close to her as possible—inside her. I wanted her to allow me the emotional and physical contact which she granted no other human being. So I waited.

I was seventeen when we first met. It was late and I had just gotten home from an eight hour shift at my part-time job at a local ski shop. Two of my friends showed up at the door with four giggling, young women. Jackie was 5'4", had long, straight dark-brown hair, and a perfect face. I struggled not to stare, but couldn't help myself.

From that night forward we slowly developed a long relationship. She became my best friend, my closest confidant, and the only person I trusted. Our lives intertwined like the stitching in a beautifully woven rug. Her family became my family, mine hers. She wore my clothes and shared my food. We even shared our money. We became as close as two people could. Our deep love and admiration for one another was built over time, the reason it was so successful.

When I was sixteen, my parents divorced. This was the hardest experience of my life. Within a week, my parents split up, my brother moved out, and I learned of my father's two year affair with a woman he now wanted to marry. I went from a secure and comfortable life style to confusion and discontent. My confidence and will to succeed both academically and socially began to drift as I slipped into a deep depression. I felt alone. If I could not trust my parents then whom could I trust?

My solution: don't cry, be strong, and never trust anyone again. I developed an attitude of complete independence, so much so that I felt untouchable. "Be emotionless," I would repeat in my head. Mr. Spock became my role model. I learned to cook for myself, earn my own spending money, and deal with life without external emotional support or guidance.

I got a job as a salesman at a local ski shop, not the most comfortable job. Day in and day out, I was forced to be warm and friendly to everyone. Although I hated the insincerity and manipulation, I was actually good at the job. Within a year I had worked my way to the top of the ski rental department, achieving a position of authority among my peers. I credit my independence and new-found feeling of invincibility to my success in the job. For an entire year I had not allowed anyone to learn my innermost thoughts. Although at times I lost friends, I was still convinced my attitude was correct. Jackie would be the only person to penetrate my barrier.

She was successful because of her patience. Although she couldn't understand my pain and anger, she continually listened and learned about me. She couldn't understand how, at seventeen, I could go days, even weeks without seeing my family, how I could essentially live alone without the security and attention a healthy family provides. Yet she persisted. She continued to date me. She was determined to reach me emotionally.

By the spring of our senior year in high school, my emotional shield was wearing thin. She began to understand me. And from this understanding developed a mutual comfort. We began to share our bodies as well as our minds. We became students learning about the wonderful world of love.

Our laboratory was her parent's den. Everything in the room served a purpose. The room itself was perfectly placed on the first floor at the back of the house, as far from her parent's bedroom as possible. The couch, which became the symbol of our lost virginity, was two wall-lengths long, wide and very soft. Next to the couch was a glass table, the only noisy fragile object, a constant reminder of the need for gentleness and control. Across the room was a television which drowned out any sounds we made. "If the couch could talk, your parents would kill us," I would say. She agreed.

Until graduation a few months away, that room played an important and exciting role in our lives. Every weekend night we would rent a movie, make dinner, and indulge in one another until we were exhausted. She would bring out feelings in me I had never known. We would bring each other close to a point of complete comfort and satisfaction. But she would not agree to have sex. She taught me most of what I knew, and, ironically, my fiercest desire was to be kept at bay. We would not go "all the way" and no end was in sight.

Despite our feelings for one another, we had developed a love at an awkward time in our lives. Summer was approaching and she would be going to Israel. In the fall we were both off to college and would be distanced by hundreds of miles. Yet we were determined to stay in love. We resisted the temptations of dating, ignored our libidos, and saved ourselves for each other. Although we did miss out on some of the wonders and excitement college had to offer, our relationship was more important.

Life was centered around weekends. Greyhound became the gateway to each other. We would spend Fridays and Sundays traveling, all for the glory of one full day together. We spent half of that day in bed talking, sleeping, and fooling around. As college life would have it, much of this was done in the company of sleeping roommates. Yet the importance of the situation outweighed concerns for privacy.

During these weekends, I repeatedly tried to convince her the time had come, yet she always prevented intercourse. "I don't feel comfortable," she would say time and again. Frustrated, I would argue that it was contradictory to allow me and want me to indulge in her body to such an extent, but not to let me "go all the way." Had I convinced her during those moments of frustration, we would have had sex against her better judgment. I would then have been selfish, manipulative and guilty of violating her emotionally and physically. My only recourse, as hard as it was, was to wait. Her comfort with me was more important.

The end of our first semester at college was near. We had proved to the world and ourselves that nothing could come between us. Four uninterrupted weeks ahead were ours to continue our mutual exploration on that wonderful brown couch in her den. We did a lot of catching up, emotionally and physically, and rekindled our vow not to be with anyone else. As Christmas break came to an end, I became increasingly frustrated. Jackie and I had fooled around almost every night. Each encounter brought us closer to making love. I wanted so much for her to agree. I wanted to know in my mind that she trusted me as much as I trusted her. Yet she always stopped me short of that critical moment. She constantly explained she wasn't ready. And I forced myself to refrain from arguing. I was frustrated, but to be frustrated over the fact that my girl friend wouldn't make love with me made very little sense. Her body and what to do with it was her decision. Who was I to dictate her life? But like most young male virgins, I was thinking of that critical, wonderful moment when she would finally let me go all the way. I would become a man in my own mind and find out what all the excitement over sex was about. And most important, I would feel at ease knowing our feelings of love and trust were mutual. I would make her feel so wonderful. She would then wonder why she had waited so long. In the end, I would be the only man allowed inside her. She would trust me completely with her body and soul. Yet this situation would not come for a long time. She was not ready. I would have to wait.

Second semester at college, our alternating weekend plan didn't always materialize as academic demands increased. Every weekend apart created more desire to be together. We were both becoming a little paranoid at the thought of the distance separating us and of possibly being seduced by another person. When we did manage to meet, we would often spend hours just talking, getting to know one another again. Time had passed, and although we had been in constant contact, seeing each other was always nerve-wracking at first. Is she not telling me something? Does she want to break up but didn't want to tell me over the phone? The thought would ring through my head, and I would later learn in hers as well.

Conversation would lead to kissing, then to fooling around. As always, we often came so close to making love that I felt she was saying yes in her own subtle way. Yet the time was still not right. She would move away, explaining that she was not ready and that I was pressuring her. And she was right. Yet rationalizing this fact against an active libido was not that easy. I was a young man of nineteen and still a virgin. My male ego was being destroyed. Didn't society dictate that a male should lose his virginity at sixteen or seventeen? I was very late. With every passing day, I felt more and more "nerd-like." Furthermore, I was scared at the thought of her not permitting me the intimacy I had allowed her. She had broken my cocoon and opened me up to the world again. Even though I was still depressed because of my family situation, she was my saving grace. I had revealed my inner thoughts to her, in spite of having promised myself I would never do so again. In my own mind, when she said she wasn't ready, I felt she didn't know if she trusted me or ever would. This made me feel insecure about our relationship. I didn't want to have her turn on me as my parents had. This constant insecurity of her hurting me was at the base of my frustration. My only recourse was to persist and have faith that she would reach the conclusion that I was the one.

As the spring semester passed, so did my frustration. I finally came to understand how unjustified and irrational it was. And with each visit, every time we fooled around, I learned to deal with the fact that I would have to stop pushing her. I had to face the fact that she had to make the next move and I was not to be part of her decision-making process.

Spring break was upon us. I had been waiting at her house for hours talking with her parents when she arrived looking great and happy to see me. After hours of talking, unpacking and eating dinner with her family, her parents went to bed and her sister went out for the evening. The den was clear for our use.

We slowly took off each other's clothes. As the hours progressed, we felt wonderful but tired from our passion. As we lay on the couch she began to ask why I had stopped pushing her to have intercourse.

"You weren't ready," I told her. "I decided you had to make the next move."

She looked at me, almost as if she was disappointed I had not persisted. "Tomorrow, I want to go buy condoms," she replied.

My heart jumped. After close to a year of waiting, Jackie was finally consenting to make love with me. She wanted to go all the way. I didn't know how to react. I had anticipated this moment for so long and was now at a loss for words. I was shocked and almost wanted to say "I'm not ready yet." But I couldn't. I had to keep calm. I couldn't let her know I was scared. If she realized this, she might have second thoughts.

The next morning we drove to the farthest and largest supermarket we knew. Variety was the key if we were to learn about contraception. And we didn't want to be recognized. Half of one aisle was covered with different varieties of condoms, vaginal creams, spermicide and other assorted contraceptive devices. We had no idea what we were looking for. Did we want extra strength with spermicide, latex without, skin with lubricant on the outside, extra wide or long? And what brand? The options were as varied as cars in a lot. We had no idea where to begin.

Our solution was to buy the most expensive and strongest condom with spermicide we could find. We figured that top quality always cost the most, and spermicide would kill any sperm that slipped through.

Paying became a new problem. The simple fact that a guy and a girl were together buying condoms meant the obvious. The checkout clerk could make her own assumptions. And although sexual intercourse was as common as cherry pie, we were extremely embarrassed at the prospect of having other people know what we were up to. Yet Jackie insisted we buy condoms and I was not going to complain. Our solution was to hide them in an array of other products. Maybe they wouldn't be noticed.

Tonight was to be the big night. Jackie and I were to lose our virginity. We were to become part of the non-virgin population. I would finally be able to show her how strongly I felt about her, not to mention experiencing an act I had only dreamed of. It was only hours away.

By nine that night, the house was empty. We were alone and free. She had consented; we had bought protection, and we loved each other. The time was perfect. We began to undress each other. The mood was tense as our sexual life was about to culminate. This night would stick in our minds for the rest of our lives.

We fooled around for hours until we both knew the next move was to indulge in what we had planned. The time had come. I opened the condom packet and pulled it out. Would it do the job? Unrolling it was an experience in itself. It was tight and felt as though it would stop my blood circulation. I rolled it as far down as I could. She was lying on the bed, naked, watching me. When I finished, she remarked that she was scared and that I should go slowly. I did. I gently began to guide myself toward her and place my body in the appropriate position. I penetrated her slowly as she held on to me with both hands. We were both in pain and not enjoying ourselves as much as we had anticipated. Yet our desire to make this situation work left no alternative but to continue. And we did. Seconds later I came and the experience ended. Blood had stained the couch and both of us were completely unsatisfied with what had transpired. Sex had turned out to be less exciting than we had imagined.

Later that night, after cleaning the couch and ourselves, we agreed that the act of sex was in fact the fullest expression of our love, and that it would get better with time. We had to practice, as one must in any endeavor. We had to learn about each other physically as we had done for so long emotionally. Then we could combine the physical and the mental to create an overall experience of complete satisfaction and love for one another.

The next day we tried again, this time using a lubricant. Again, our efforts were invaded by pain and mistrust of the condom. But we came closer to enjoying ourselves. And with every future encounter, our love became more fulfilling. We had waited four days short of a year, but Jackie's patience, my patience, and a strong mutual love sustained us.

26

Despite a Harvard Education

by Jacqueline Walsh

When panting sighs the bosom fill,
And hands by chance united thrill
At once with one delicious pain
The pulses and the nerves of twain;
When eyes that erst could meet with ease,
Do seek, yet, seeking, shyly shun
Ecstatic conscious unison,
—The sure beginnings, say, be these,
Prelusive to the strain of love
Which angels sing in heaven above?

Or is it but the vulgar tune,
Which all that breathe beneath the moon
So accurately learn—so soon?

— A.H. Clough

We met for lunch some six years after our first encounter, and as we were saying goodbye in the parking lot he asked, by the way, could I help find a priest to officiate at his wedding? Being eager at that time to do almost anything to please a man, I agreed. I gave him my cloak, too, and added that I would be honored to bake the wedding cake as my gift. I got into my car, watched him dwindle in my rear-view mirror, and, to my intense irritation and surprise, began to cry. I had been torn apart by Brian many times, and believed myself to be triumphantly healed—but scar tissue can prove more delicate than it tries to appear.

Yes, this is a story of first sex, loss of virginity, but more than that, it is a story of first love, and the shattering of elusive, illusive romantic hope. The intensity of my feelings then and in the years after that time stem far more from the latter issue than the former; many men since have rolled off of my consciousness with almost worrisome ease, while the memory of this one clings with powerful tenacity.

Slightly more than a decade has passed since our initial encounter, yet its details remain burned into my mind more distinctly than much of what I did last week. It was the middle of my freshman fall at college, a pretty October weekend during which a friend from school was staying with me. We had no particular plans, but Mona had promised to say hi to another friend while she was in town. We found him and a friend of his, Brian, in their residential dining hall, and joined them for lunch. I do not recall lightning bolts, but the chemistry between Brian and me was quickly evident, at least to me; he seemed at once to be everything I could have ever wanted and that my family valued: tall, dark, and handsome, educated, athletic, and kind. Better still, his brother was a good friend of Mona's and mine at school, and so I grew to assume that the sterling character and integrity of the one I knew would be true of the other I had just met. Mona and I found ourselves that afternoon standing on the sidelines of a playing field, their team jackets draped about our shoulders. We all had dinner together and decided to go see "Live and Let Die" playing on campus that evening. At the movie, I was thrilled when he embraced my knee with his hand as he laughed, and then kept it there.

After the credits had rolled, we trooped off to Brian's room, where they introduced me to various drinking games (I was not new to alcohol, but was essentially uninterested in it, also a little afraid, having seen its horrors for many years). This did not lead where one might think, for the games soon disbanded, and I recall my faculties being on red alert. We did, however, eventually turn out the lights, lay a fire, and split into pairs, Mona and her friend (just buddies, by the way), lying on the couch, and me and Brian on the floor by the hearth. He lay behind and pressed up against me, holding and stroking me for a long time, delicately. As an aesthetic counterpoint, the rock song by Kiss, "I Was Made For Loving You," strained out from its hushed volume, its guitar pace insistent. Brian whisperingly indicated that we should slide off to his bedroom, extending his hand to help me up. I arose, conscious of my audience on the couch and now suddenly confused about how I should proceed.

My primary concern towering above all else was to guarantee the relationship, to ensure that he would want to stay with me always. Sex, I assumed, would effect such an assurance, would be either a symbol of our bond or its creator, possibly both. Put crudely, it was using sex to get love, as the cliché goes. I knew that I wanted to go to bed with him, and soon, but that particular moment seemed poorly timed: I had no contraceptives with me at all, and dared not discuss it for fear that any such mundane discourse would "spoil the magic," ruin the momentum or make him reconsider and leave. I wanted to risk neither losing him nor getting pregnant, and so, following him the few feet down the hall, my mind scrambled furiously for a course of action and an explanation I could offer.

Standing just inside his bedroom door, he embraced me firmly, warmly, leisurely. I had decided by then on the rhythm method for the first time, believing that after that I would have my "forever man" and then we could mutually agree on a better solution. I had also realized where I was in my predictable cycle and knew I could not risk anything that night, but would come back several days later, just before my period when it was "safe." Just as I was forming in my head a way to tell him I could not make love that night but would be sure to do so later, I noticed that my body no longer shivered with novel touch but decidedly shook with—fear? I wasn't sure, and still don't know, but I couldn't control it. I ended up explaining as soothingly as possible that I was just really, really tired and wanted only to curl up with him and go to sleep (his clock glowed 2:00). Happily, he agreed without any contrary insistence and with gentle, understanding smiles and caresses. Fully clothed, we slept, with him holding me tight. His willingness to let me do that further cemented my trust in him; when Mona and I left on Sunday, I had already resolved to return later in the week.

* * *

As early as eighth grade I entertained fantasies of meeting "The One" who would be my perfect man, the soul mate who would make my life complete. Beginning in high school, I became hyper-vigilant at every new class, activity meeting, concert, church gathering, and social event, sure that at any time my eyes would meet with the man of my destiny. It would be difficult, perhaps impossible, to overdramatize the desperate intensity of my searching at this time, indeed, for many years to come. Such sentiments grew, predictably, out of a textbook broken home early childhood sprinkled with alcohol, a father distant in all possible ways, a mother with a seriously problematic history with men, and an abysmal self-image. I thought my value was determined by my appearance and by having a man who wanted me. These feelings also grew out of intense explorations in high school into various spiritualities, from a conventional high church Episcopalianism to several esoteric paths. I was tutored when I was overseas during the two summers preceding my entrance into college by a woman whose whole life was spirituality; I believed myself to have acquired an especially profound and enlightened understanding of myself and of love. I could explain, in a way I thought articulate and convincing, how one needed to let one's self go into the will of God in order to be free, and it was at these moments of letting go that love came. And come it would, for my astrological birth chart decreed that marriage would center powerfully in my life, and that I would know the man very soon. As a parting prophecy just before I left for college, my mother, whose every word may as well have been God's to me at that time, said that she knew I would meet someone very special that year. This she said with the lilting wink that promised everything.

When I first sat down across the dining room table from Brian, I decided that he could be that man. As we talked, and I learned more of him, I grew surer and surer. He seemed to fulfill every premonition and aspiration I had ever had. I was ecstatic, overcome that I should be so blessed, in awe that someone this terrific would want me, of all people.

It was a peculiar tightrope, then, that first evening, knowing that this was to be, a given, indeed a gift, and that I therefore did not have to work on or manipulate it. But I knew also that I had to not make any mistakes, and neither push nor deny him in such a way as to drive him off. Leaving him the next day, I thought very carefully about when I should return, late enough to be "safe" and to not appear too demanding, soon enough to capitalize on the momentum already set. I decided that the following Thursday would be perfect.

* * *

I did not telephone first, but just showed up at his door in the very early evening. His roommate answered, and let me in, explaining that Brian was still in the shower following a game. He invited me to sit down and went down the hall to alert Brian who came out almost immediately, dripping wet and almost wearing a towel. He smiled broadly, said he was so happy I had come, and would I just wait for him to dry and dress? Of course. He returned, sat right next to me on the couch, held my hand, caressed my leg. I felt enormously thrilled that he still seemed so eager to be with me, that the events and emotions of the precious weekend were not a mistake in either of our minds. We went down to the basement to shoot a little pool, have a beer, and get his laundry.

The beer is important for its singularity; he would later claim to have been drunk, but this is an untenable assertion. I assume that he celebrated in the usual manner following that afternoon's game, but its effects had to have been negligible by the time we went back up to his bedroom to put the laundry away that night. I, in any case, never finished even the one bottle offered me, a fact due partly to conscious decision.

Perhaps an hour later, we were back upstairs. A single desk lamp illuminated the small room as we sat on his bed with a pile of socks and T-shirts; it was not long before those lay on the floor, slowly pushed aside. Oddly, the clothes on our bodies were displaced as little as possible. Indeed, the more I reflect on it, the more telling I find it that I was stripped of only what was necessary, and he removed nothing, only lowering his jeans a little at the last moment. The two layers of cotton between our hearts came to symbolize in my mind an ironic and nearly impenetrable barrier for real intimacy.

I don't know how I felt, and don't think I did then. I certainly tried to act confident, and wasn't shaking this time, though I seem to recall a certain physical and psychic numbness. What tipped him off was a fairly firm resistance; he stopped almost immediately, and asked quietly, without raising his head to look at me, "Are you a virgin?" I said yes, and there was quite a pause. He answered, "The first time should be with someone you really love." I said I didn't know it wasn't, and added something, which I can't quote exactly, about time as such not being necessary, love at first sight, et cetera. And so he proceeded, but the tone of the encounter altered entirely; tender passion had turned joyless and mechanical.

Although it did not hurt as much as I expected, pleasure was certainly not even a remote possibility. But I revelled in the knowledge that I was being bound to him, for the physical union surely was emblematic of a higher and deeper, possibly eternal, connection as well. I later discovered that I had in fact been badly torn up and somehow was mercifully, if temporarily, unfeeling.

There was one particularly peculiar moment when he stopped and sat back a bit. I assured him with what I hoped was a convincing manner that it was all right and really didn't hurt, to which he responded that that wasn't what he was worried about. There was a pause, some fumbling, and then he resumed, with my encouragement. I never had the nerve to ask what that was about, and couldn't see well enough to verify what I suspected later, that he was putting on a condom. We never discussed or even mentioned contraception; I just made sure to myself that I was in the clear in order to spare him any inconvenience.

I should explain at this point that my use of a calendar method had nothing to do with any religious perspective. I could not get a medical appointment in time for the only two methods I would really have trusted and which would have been discreet or uninterruptive (pill and diaphragm), and I refused to consider over-the-counter alternatives as disruptive, messy, and so back-seat-of-the-car. Further, although I knew then that I would not continue to count on my reliability, I figured I could get away with it that once, an incredible notion coming from someone who apparently owes her own existence to such an idea. In any case, we may have had protection, or we may not have, and I'm not sure. He was so distant and hidden from me in nearly every way possible that I had no indication anymore that he was enjoying himself or me, or, for that matter, even had an orgasm at all; I recall largely a motion which seemed, eventually and almost arbitrarily, to end. Then stillness and continued silence.

After a long while, he sat back on his heels and said evenly, "You'd better get your clothes on now. I'll walk you home." I raised myself up, beginning to feel deeply sad and confused about why everything had suddenly gone so wrong. He clicked on the light to reveal, to my initial embarrassment, a significant quantity of blood on his blanket, which I knew might happen but didn't think would or had. Brian, having pulled up his pants, disappeared wordlessly into the bathroom. As I was looking at the brilliant stain, reflecting both bitterly and reverently on that which was shed for him, he returned with a beer mug full of cold water which he dumped with sacrilegious indifference onto the scarlet.

Only a couple of hours after I entered the building, I found myself leaving in disbelief, my escort dutifully alongside but at a slight distance, both hands shoved firmly into his pockets. I assume we made small-talk during the five minute walk, but I have no memory of substance. What I do remember is arriving inside my dormitory living room, a brief kiss on the cheek, and (I am not making this up) the assurance that he would still like to be friends and that he would call me. Then the closed door. I went into my room and sat in a tight ball in the corner on my bed, dressed, lights on, staring and trying just to grasp the simple facts of what had happened.

After two weeks I had not heard from him, of course, and though I knew perfectly well what to make of that, I called him anyway to ask, very shyly and haltingly, if he had any interest in continuing the relationship as we had started it. His answer was predictable, at once cruel and polite; he explained that he had a girlfriend back home to whom he had a certain obligation. I thanked him for his honesty, and put the phone down. I think it was then that I cried for the first time. Still, he had said he wanted to try to be friends, and I believed him, so I arranged a couple of opportunities for him to come over to my room so we could talk and get to know one another better. I admit that I hoped a certain seduction could take place, but he sat on my desk shifting as though he could hardly wait to leave. These meetings proved only awkward and enormously painful for me, but I tried to be as friendly and accepting and forgiving as possible in the hope that one day he would be free of his girlfriend and we could resume the glorious path to shared life I thought was supposed to be ours. That vision was to explode one afternoon the following February, and though I would later share his bed a few more times, my faith in him lay then amidst irreparable rubble.

On Valentine's Day a few months later, Mona came down to visit again. I wanted to make some acknowledgement of the date but in a non-threatening way, so I bought some white freesia in a pretty vase and went to his dorm with Mona in the middle of the day to deliver it. He was out, but a roommate let us in; Mona stayed in the living room while I went into his bedroom to arrange the flowers on his desk and prepare a friendly note. As I sat to write, I saw lying out in plain view on the middle of the desk a letter in his writing; a phrase caught my eye. I was as wrong to read the first few paragraphs as he was to write them. They described the assorted pleasures various women were all too happy to provide him and which he was all too happy to receive, save for the efforts of "one freshman who just didn't understand the idea of a one-night stand." So much for the I'm-sorry-I-really-care-but-I-already-have-a-girlfriend-but-otherwise . . . story. I briefly considered drawing a heart in blood on his pillow, but instead just gathered the flowers, and left with all the composure I could muster. My tight and bloodless face apparently was not lost on his roommate, for Brian called later and we met in my room for a heated argument.

The full weight of the betrayal struck me, and struck hard, It was then that I plunged into a period of frenzied desperation which would persist chronically for over a year, and sporadically for several beyond that. I became further entrenched in various methods of coping both with this specific devastation and with a personal and family history of which this particular situation was in some ways just another symptom. These methods, some helpful, some destructive, included reclusive behavior, agonized and tearful screaming at God, eating problems, obsessive pursuit of physical fitness, some drinking, and, later, a certain degree of promiscuity. In my singular and unswerving obsession—and I do not use that word lightly—with this man, I cultivated among other things a fascinated identification with Sarah Woodruff, the "French Lieutenant's Woman," who seemed simultaneously a wronged victim of a callous and unworthy man, and a woman far beyond her lover in complexity, maturity, and strength. I admired her look over her shoulder at the character Charles Smithson, her sorrowed expression haunted and hunted, but then lancing, devastating, and turning away. I, too, wanted to be fascinating, desirable, yet unattainable; to be unfathomable and unfindable, to gain distance as I tried to clarify for myself what she could not articulate either; "it is not to be explained."

My efforts at accepting a permanently crushed vision were not helped by the fact that he called the following fall, my sophomore year, to invite me to a party. I went, expecting nothing and trying not to pay much attention to him. But he pulled me up from my conversation on the couch, and the way he danced with me communicated in no uncertain terms what he was interested in doing. He suggested we leave and go back to my room. My hopes once again rose as we undressed each other; I even had acquired a diaphragm to have just in case. Everything was wonderful until, after several minutes, he pulled back and hovered over me on hands and knees, his head hanging, and silent. After a few moments he said that this was a great mistake, that we could never let this happen again. He dressed and left.

Amazingly, by my junior year and his senior year, we were able at last to start feeling comfortable with each other as friends; I had, with great efforts of various kinds done a lot of healing, calming down, and building of confidence, and he had effected changes in his life which certainly benefitted him. We exchanged warm and sincere promises to stay in touch after his graduation, which we kept all too literally at the beginning of the following fall when I went to visit him at graduate school. This time, however, was not declared a deplorable mistake and left us both, I think, reasonably happy. But still I cried as I drove away, knowing what was never to be possible and lamenting the walls I had erected to protect myself from feeling too much. After that, there were several occasions, when we had dinner or I dropped in for a visit on my commute, which promised to lead farther than living circumstances could permit. Despite the nearly unbroken history of painful let-downs, I almost certainly would have gone along had that been possible, wishing with all my heart that at last it could work.

* * *

You would think that I would have learned my lesson after the first time, certainly the second, and would not have kept coming back for more. But that is precisely the point: one can have securely in one's intellectual arsenal a thorough grasp of facts, of "objective" analysis, of the logical, sound choices, yet one can be at the very same time utterly powerless actually to act on that knowledge. A battalion of forces far more powerful than the intellect come into play at crucial moments, and impulses stemming from a multitude of subtle, complex, and not readily identifiable sources can win the day. As Paul explains in Romans 7:15-18, "I do not understand my own actions. For I do not do what I want, but I do the very thing I hate. . . . I can will what is right, but I cannot do it." In other words, I knew very well all the detailed facts about contraception, diseases, morals, decision-making, how to avoid men with problems, how to care for one's self and not make harmful decisions or get into destructive situations, and so forth. I realized over the course of several encounters that not only was sex not an especially effective way to keep a man, it was likely to backfire altogether and drive him off. I could give great advice along these lines to friends, and had I been observing myself, would have been shocked and made strenuous efforts to talk me out of this pattern of behavior. Yet I persisted and always returned, inner voices protesting but ignored.

A breakthrough occurred when I was in graduate school and studying a program which was vocationally and intellectually relevant to me, and which also had the fortunate added advantages of allowing me private opportunity to explore my past and my mind and spirit, and to move through and beyond areas where I was hurting and stalled. Among my areas of study were obsessions and destructive disorders, and issues of self-control and self-care placed in a psychological and theological context. During this time, I was for the first time able to say no, and not once but twice. I was visiting him again for dinner, and when I prepared to leave, he asked me to stay and began kissing me invitingly. I withdrew a little, smiled with genuine affection, and said that I really needed to go home now. Which I did. The next day, each of us wrote a letter to the other, apologizing and realizing or explaining that the friendship shouldn't be jeopardized in that manner again. On another occasion, again at his house for dinner, I was offered a couch for the night so I would not have to drive the forty-five minutes home. The sexual promise was not immediately explicit here, but we had tried to sleep on separate beds before and it had never worked. Much as I still found him extremely attractive and loved him very much, I knew we would never be ultimately right for one another, and I was weary of painful scenarios; we hugged goodbye and I drove away feeling peaceful and sure although, I confess, with vestiges of regret lingering still.

The difficulty is that I cannot articulate precisely what it was that finally made the difference and gave me the self-assurance or self-love to say no, I don't need to do this to myself any more, I'm worth more than that. Or rather, I do see that it is those very things, a sense of being valuable and lovable that is firmly grasped by my being, that gives me the freedom to stop searching in the wrong trees for a sense of self-worth. But I question how much real good my explanation can be in terms of concrete impact on anyone else's actions: I envision many heads like mine nodding in solemn agreement and comprehension, and then the very same people proceeding as I did to plunge into similarly disastrous situations. I understood those principles when I was sixteen, but was not able even to begin actually to live them for many years, and I still have a ways to go. There is no question that I had to fall flat on my face, not once but over and over again with many more men, before the reality of self-hatred took on concrete and therefore unavoidable form, and before such lofty book knowledge, as I had, solidified into substantive and practical value.

27

Condoms, Failure Rates, and the "M" Word

by Mary H. Devaney, Director
Parents for Prevention

In most HIV/AIDS prevention programs and pamphlets directed toward young people, abstinence from sexual intercourse and monogamy are mentioned, but the emphasis is clearly on "safer sex practices" and promotion of the universal use of condoms. You will never see or hear the dreaded "M" word MORALITY. Actually, on occasion, an individual who dares to question the wisdom of condom availability in the schools may be disparagingly referred to as a MORALIST.

Granted, the statement, "Condoms are not 100 percent effective," is always made. However, the time spent on effectiveness is non-existent in comparison with the time spent on "safer sex," and condom training, motivation, promotion, and negotiation. Why is this? Young people, adolescents, are currently being infected with HIV in greater numbers than any other group in the nation. This is expected to continue. What exactly does "not 100 percent" mean? The truth is that behind this benign sounding, seemingly insignificant warning, there is an abundance of troubling data. Prior to the onset of HIV/AIDS, condom failure was not a cause of great concern. Then, FAILURE WAS NEVER FATAL. Now, the playing field has changed.

In 1987, the *Journal of the American Medical Association* and the *New England Journal of Medicine* published the results of studies of HIV transmission in couples. In separate studies, conducted over several years, Dr. Margaret Fischl and Dr. James Goedert came to the same conclusion. There is no "safe sex" with an HIV infected partner. In those couples who abstained from sexual intercourse, no uninfected partners became HIV positive. Those who had "unprotected intercourse," without condoms, infected their partners approximately 82 percent of the time. Those who routinely used condoms infected their partners approximately 17 percent of the time. These tests were continued for many years, and the 17 percent infection rate held up. Sometimes infection did not take place until after four years of condom use as a method of prevention. Why? Precision and exactness are impossible in this type of study, so many conclusions depend on conjecture. HIV-infected persons become more infectious as the virus reproduces and destroys the immune system. This, in combination with the unpredictable, random nature of condom failure, is the probable explanation.

The following are major causes of condom breakage and failure:

1. Improper use, human error
2. Improper storage by truckers during transport, by retailers, and by consumers
3. Quality control problems of the condom industry
4. Manufacturing defects

Of course, in the studies of HIV transmission in couples, infection was reduced from 82 percent to 17 percent. Is this adequate when the result is a prolonged, painful death? Abstinence from sexual intercourse is 100 percent effective. Depending on condoms for protection has the same odds as Russian Roulette, one in six.

A 27.9 percent condom failure rate for pregnancy among teenage girls was reported in the January/February, 1992 issue of *Family Planning Perspectives*. These young people had received both counseling and instruction from the research arm of Planned Parenthood, the Alan Guttmacher Institute. Why was their failure rate so high? Again, we must depend on conjecture. In combination with the major causes of condom failure, we are dealing with adolescents whose bodies and minds are still in a state of transition. Psychologically, teenagers are present and pleasure oriented; they feel invincible; they take risks. Teachers and parents can attest to their lack of forethought and preparedness. Their changing bodies have unpredictable hormone levels, unpredictable reaction and performance in the area of sexual intercourse. In the same issue of Family Planning Perspectives cited above, a study of adult couples resulted in a condom slippage and breakage rate of 14.6 percent. Researchers commented on pages 22 and 23:

> "If they are accurate, these rates indicate a sobering level of exposure to the risk of pregnancy and infection with HIV or other STDs even among those who consistently use condoms."

"Most disturbing of all is the fact that ten years into the AIDS epidemic, we have so little understanding of the efficacy of condoms during use."

The Alan Guttmacher Institute was reported in *USA Today,* March 26, 1992, as having found that condom failure varies widely according to age and marital status. Adult women had a failure rate of 14.8 percent, those under twenty 25.9 percent. Extensive studies by *Consumer Reports* were published in their March, 1989, issue. Researchers found that among condom brands, and among different types of condoms within those brands, there were a variety of failure rates. A federally funded study at UCLA demonstrated that some major condom brands leaked the HIV virus from 10 to 25 percent of the time. In September, 1989, this was reported in the *Los Angeles Times* by Alan Parachini who obtained the 1,000 page report under the Freedom of Information Act.

Included in most HIV prevention literature and presentations is a recommendation that non-oxynol 9 and other spermicides provide, or "may provide," additional protection. This assumption is based on a clinical study which was refuted, or at least put into question, by a study in the field. At the Fifth International Aids Conference, held in Montreal, June 4-9, 1989, the results of a study of prostitutes in Nairobi was presented. Those who used non-oxynol 9 had an infection rate of 55 percent as opposed to 45 percent among placebo users. Why? Once more we are in the realm of conjecture. Did the spermicide cause an allergic reaction in the infected prostitutes? Did they have lesions or other STDs? Did the spermicide undergo phase conversion causing a change in the acidity required for effectiveness? Absolute answers are not possible, but, certainly all of the information available should be taken into consideration if condoms are to be counted on to prevent HIV infection.

Finally, in the *American Journal of Public Health,* January, 1988, Paul J. Feldblum, M.S.P.H., and Judith A. Fortnew, PhD., published a comprehensive review of the literature relating to condoms, spermicides, and the transmission of HIV. They conclude on page 52:

> "There exists the widespread assumption that condoms, and possibly spermicides can effectively prevent infection with HIV. **The evidence, for this assumption, however, is not strong.**"

So . . . what we have is a numbers game. Or is it a shell game? Clearly, the "condoms are not 100 percent effective" statement does not honestly reflect the available data. In the case of teenagers, at this time our primary concern, failure rates are more accurately represented as falling somewhere between 14 and 27.9 percent. These figures are for pregnancy, which can happen only a few days per month. The HIV virus is much smaller than a sperm and can transmit 365 days per year. If condoms are to be depended on to protect from HIV infection, all available data must be considered.

No matter where the truth lies in these studies and statistics, we are playing a dangerous game. If current STD prevalence among young people is an indicator of what to expect as HIV becomes more widespread, we are in for a nightmare. Each year, two-thirds of the twelve million cases of venereal disease which occur are found in those under age twenty-five. Chlamydia, herpes simplex II, HPV (venereal warts), syphilis, and gonorrhea are considered epidemic among the young. These diseases are found among high school age students in prosperous communities as well as in the inner cities, among college students as well as the disadvantaged.

What is the solution? What alternatives do we have? At the moment the dominant educational philosophy is to downplay condom failure and promote universal condom use. We cannot plan on a vaccine or cure for HIV/AIDS for years to come, if ever. We must concentrate on prevention.

Perhaps we will have to return to the MORALIST who opposed condom promotion in the schools. Perhaps he was not trying to impose his annoying values on others. Perhaps he realized that if we do not create a new, health-oriented, social norm of self-discipline and restraint in matters of sexual behavior, we may lose an entire generation.

28

Hurricane Helen

by Stuart Ellis

My first experience occurred during spring break of my senior year in college, when I took a short leave from my classes, my senses, and my set of beliefs I had carefully constructed since early adolescence. I was 21 years old.

During high school, I had firmly established a lifestyle appropriate for someone preparing to become a Puritan minister—no alcohol, no drugs, no women. However, I did not abstain because of any moral or religious strictures. I grew up in a progressive household. My parents had never made a big issue of experimenting with sex, drugs, or alcohol. They had spoken to me several times about using "my best judgment," and reinforced that they trusted me to make the right decisions. However, I was not thinking about these activities at all. I virtually ignored social situations and instead focused on my academic and athletic goals which became the center of my life.

There were also some secondary factors involved in establishing my straightlaced lifestyle. I had strongly negative impressions of drug-users acquired during elementary school. When our teachers showed us movies and slides of unkempt individuals using substances, these impressions took hold. From that point on, I linked drug use in general with the stigma of unwashed, scraggly hippies living idly in communes or wandering around city streets.

I never liked the taste of alcohol either, and so could not see the logic in spending several dollars for the privilege of drinking something that tasted like turpentine; I had much more enjoyment downing a coke.

Finally, women simply could not compete with all my other interests and hobbies. I had a couple of short-lived relationships during high school. During college I became involved in two long-distance relationships which, of course, were very easy to relegate to the bottom of the priority list. During my senior year, this list included ROTC, political debate club, teaching, music, and performing.

By the time I had nearly completed college, my lifestyle choices had become firmly established. I believed my achievements occurred in part because I had eliminated extraneous things, such as girlfriends, from my life.

As I began my final semester, the ROTC program which had provided me with a full academic scholarship, notified me that instead of deferring my active duty service obligation until after medical school, they were placing me in the infantry branch immediately after graduation. It was the shock of my life. I had neither the aptitude not the temperament for the infantry. I had dreamed of going to medical school since junior high, and I felt like the next four and a half years of my life were about to be snatched from me.

I was totally numb as I began my final semester, counting down the months until school ended and my "jail sentence" began. Sleepwalking through classes, I became totally fixated on my future life as an infantry officer. The only time I was ever connected to the world outside my thoughts was during weekly performances as a member of my university's hallowed musical performing group.

Spring break arrived with impeccable timing in late February as winter had worn its welcome. For the members of our performing group, spring break meant only one thing: "TOUR"—nearly two weeks of travel, performances, and intense bonding among the members of our all-male group. This group, steeped in tradition, was sent across the country each year as heavyweight fundraisers to remind alumni of their fondest college memories.

I viewed senior year "Tour" as my last chance to really enjoy myself before my life was to be transformed by Uncle Sam. My personal goal was total immersion and participation in the related festivities.

Our trip encompassed the Southeast. By the time we reached Charlotte, I had detached myself from the world of school and was swept up in the mania of the experience.

Three days later we arrived in New Orleans for a performance hosted by the local alumni club. We turned in a typical show—very loose, full of improvisation, but also filled with energy. It was always great fun to perform in new cities before fresh faces.

The performance ended by 9:30 that evening, leaving plenty of time to enjoy the city. We headed to none other than the French Quarter and Pat

O'Brien's, home of the legendary drink, The Hurricane. It is a syrupy sweet drink which tastes like a thick glass of Hawaiian Punch, but has the effect of a Mike Tyson punch.

Due to the early hour, we avoided the customary 90 minute wait and were seated immediately. Everyone in the contingent ordered a hurricane. The waiter finally turned to me and asked if I was going to make it a clean sweep. The others began to chuckle and smirk, as everyone waited for me to order my traditional coke. But that night was not going to be normal for me.

I was experiencing one of those Fred Flintstone moments when faced with a very important moral decision. The "good" Fred, halo and all, and the "bad Fred" with the requisite horns would appear on either shoulder and goad him to choose either the virtuous or the less-than-virtuous path.

I am not making any excuses, but I think it was the exotic location, the feeling of freedom associated with spring break, and my overriding desire to make this a truly memorable tour that caused me to obey the bad Fred. At that moment, I began my night of "oh-what-the-hell," as I violated my abstinence and ordered a hurricane.

By the time the drinks arrived I was very thirsty and took large sips through the straw. Detecting no unpleasant taste, I underestimated the alcoholic content and downed the drink in under three minutes. When I had quenched my thirst chewing on the remaining ice, I realized no one else had made a dent in his drink. In fact, they were all sipping their hurricanes like after-dinner liqueurs.

I hadn't eaten since noon and hadn't built any tolerance to alcohol over my years of abstinence, so within five minutes I was feeling very good and very cocky. In fact, I was feeling so cocky that when someone produced a pot pipe and passed it my way, instead of my customary "no thanks," I accepted.

I had never touched pot before, but at that moment wasn't repelled by the thought—only very, very curious. I decided that if I were going to try it this one time, I wasn't going to take just one puff and feel any hollow placebo effect. Rather, I wanted the actual physical experience of being stoned. With that, I took 6 or 7 puffs and held my breath each time I inhaled. Then I waited.

After five minutes, the euphoria arrived. I suddenly loved everyone, deemed every member of the performing group to be a blood relative or long, lost friend. When I had finished hugging and kissing all the cast members and showing off some recently-learned choreography to the other patrons of Pat O'Brien's, I exited the bar and took my act to the streets of the French Quarter.

I was feeling very pleased with myself and loudly sang my way back to the hotel. Arriving in my room, I lay down and began to experience a sort of disembodiment, as though I couldn't feel my limbs because they were asleep. I got up to relieve myself, and, while standing in the bathroom, had an even stranger thought—that I was using someone else's equipment to relieve myself. I woke both my roommates and demanded they observe this phenomenon.

They promptly threw me out, so I wandered the hotel hallways and ran into a huge party being thrown by the University of Mississippi marching band, in town for a college band festival. I was very relaxed and in great spirits and chatted with several people including a saxophone player who appeared quite interested in my origins and the nature of my performing group. She questioned with abundant confidence and consumed each answer with equal delight. I also vividly recall her porcelain skin and smiling eyes.

As she began to tell of her background and hometown on the Gulf, it became difficult to converse over the loud party music and she asked if I wanted to go to her room and watch Letterman. Ordinarily, this type of invitation would have paralyzed me with indecision, and I would have contemplated all the ramifications, but not that night. Once again, I was very, very curious. Upon arriving in her room, I performed a very dramatic swan-dive onto her bed, and she followed suit.

After we finished comparing dives, she turned on the TV, and before Letterman was finished with his last Stupid Pet Trick (dog attacking vacuum cleaner), I was receiving a shoulder massage. By the time Letterman began his nightly Top 10 list, she began lightly kissing the back of my neck. Before I knew it, I wasn't watching television anymore.

Indeed, this was a very strange situation for me, as I had never kissed anyone whom I had only recently met, and she certainly qualified. I consider kissing someone to be a very personal act and had never felt comfortable "making out" before getting to know the person. Yet, on this occasion it never occurred to me to object.

I'm sure that by this time any purely physiological effects of my first encounter with pot and alcohol had worn off, but that strange disembodied sensation remained; I felt as if I were standing on the other side of the room watching myself kissing this unfamiliar person.

I continued to "watch" the two of us as the action proceeded below the waist. Traditionally, I would have become alarmed at this point, because this was **very** intimate territory for me, reserved strictly for girlfriends, not hallway acquaintances. However, instead of becoming uncomfortable, I was feeling somewhat amused and very curious to see what would happen next. So I became passive, allowing her to set the agenda. As she made further moves, I began to wonder if she intended to stop, or if this was indeed going to become an even more memorable evening.

I also had another thought—"if things **do** progress further, am I carrying any protection?" No sooner had I begun to take a serious mental inventory of my wallet's contents than she reached over to some sort of carry-on luggage by the bed and searched through a plastic bag. After putting the bag away, she turned to me and said playfully, "Can you believe Student Health Services was giving these away in their 'Spring Break Travel Packs?'" She said she especially liked the animated duck on the wrapper and the assortment of colors.

I looked at the condom as upon a foreign object (indeed, I had only previously seen them inside the wrapper and was not familiar with the intricacies of their assembly and use.) She laughed and assisted me with the task, which I found tested the very limits of my motor coordination.

After overcoming that hurdle, I was content to become passive again, and found having sex for the first time to be a warm, cozy, and comfortable experience. I still did not quite believe it was happening, but enjoyed the experience nonetheless.

The evening ended with another hour or so of sharing childhood and hometown anecdotes. Finally, at around 4:00 AM we exchanged addresses and said good night. I returned to my room.

"Losing it" did not transform my life; nor did it mark the beginning of a string of one-night stands. Rather, the experience helped me remove an artificial barrier I had constructed which prevented me from experiencing any type of physical intimacy.

In a more general sense, I learned that night that it is okay to "let go" sometimes and relax certain inhibitions, providing I use decent judgment. I found I could violate my self-imposed prohibitions, and the world would not collapse around me as a result.

I've never been drunk or stoned since, but now I have a more realistic impression of the effects of pot or alcohol. They are no longer the mysterious substances of my adolescence, and consequently, I have lost the curiosity I used to feel about them. Also, as I have grown into full adulthood, sex has become a natural corollary to establishing an intimate relationship rather than something to obsess over and fear.

29

With a Little Help from My Friends

by Bea Graham

I left my virginity with a man named Paul. He was twenty-two; I was fourteen. We were introduced by my friend Kate. I was with Kate and her boyfriend, Jake. Paul lived in his own apartment which he shared with his friend Rick.

I didn't see him again until couple of weeks later at a party at my house. My parents were away. I was pleased he had come. He and his friends were the oldest members of my illicit high school gathering. My friends were as impressed as I.

Paul was handsome and soft spoken. I was flattered by his attention. As the evening wound down people began to leave. Paul stayed. Alone together we started kissing fully clothed, I had a bunk bed, so there wasn't much room. As he stroked my body, I started to stroke him, following his lead, my hand hesitating just at his pelvis. I had never touched a penis and wasn't sure I wanted to. As I stroked his thigh and his stomach he whispered gently to me, "it won't bite." Of course it won't, I realized, relieved. Cautiously, I touched him.

"I hope this is OK; I've never done it before." It wasn't until this moment that he understood I was a virgin and had little experience with guys. He was sweet and got a bit nervous himself. He called me "baby" and made me feel like a woman. He said we didn't have to do anything else, but it hadn't occurred to me that anything else would happen. We continued to caress each other with our clothes on and eventually fell asleep.

I don't remember specific details after that first night. We saw each other on weekends for about three months always at his place. My parents didn't ask me where I was staying. We slept in the same bed, showered together and fooled around, but we didn't have sex. I wasn't sure. I knew losing my virginity was an important decision and that I would always remember that person. I didn't really know what to base my decision on. I had it in my mind that I wanted to stay a virgin until I was sixteen, but I knew if I waited Paul wouldn't be the one. I figured that a twenty-two year old guy wouldn't stay with a girl without sex. I never actually asked him.

I finally decided I wanted Paul as my first lover. I didn't talk my decision over with anyone. I thought he was kind, gentle, and most of all extremely attractive. I felt important being with him. My family, for the most part, ignored me while Paul paid attention to me. I remember thinking, even if it was a disaster, when I looked back at least it would be to a handsome face. I'd be proud to show my own children a photo. My two best friends, Kate and Charlotte, both a year ahead of me in school, were already having sex. They didn't pressure me, but their being sexually active made it seem okay.

I asked my mother to take me to the gynecologist for a diaphragm fitting. She took me without asking why, though she had met my boyfriend and knew he was twenty-two. Later on she said she thought I wanted a diaphragm just to have it, so I could feel more adult, the way a child has a pair of heels or make-up to play with.

Paul and Rick were giving a party. I stayed over at my best friend Charlotte's house the night before. We went out for dinner with her parents, and afterwards I practiced putting my diaphragm in. Charlotte stood outside the bathroom door asking how I was doing as I carefully followed my gynecologist's directions and the diagram in the case. Once I had it down, Charlotte and I went for a walk so I could get used to wearing it.

We went to the party together. Charlotte, Kate, Kate's boyfriend, Jake and I were the youngest guests. Paul was friends with Jake's older brother. I was excited and happy. Paul's friends seemed close, like a family, a family without parents. I was part of this family and my two best friends were with me. They both knew I planned to lose my virginity that night. We giggled. We danced. We glowed.

The party died down. Kate hugged me, wished me good luck and she and Jake went back to his mother's apartment a few floors below. I knew Charlotte had thought Rick was cute since she'd first met him. Everyone left except Paul, Rick, Charlotte and me.

I had told Paul I was getting a diaphragm. We went into his room and got undressed. Charlotte stayed with Rick. I told Paul that I had the diaphragm with me.

"Where," he wanted to know.

"On," I said.

The night before, when Charlotte and I went for a walk, she had explained the important details to me. It would hurt a little at first; I might bleed; and afterwards the guy falls asleep right away. So I felt prepared. She was in the next room. Kate was a few floors away. We would all have sex that night. Would it be at the same time?

Sure enough everything Charlotte mentioned happened. When Paul fell asleep I knew things had gone well. I hugged my body wondering what about me had changed. I curled up next to him and fell asleep. A few hours later I woke to him kissing and stroking me again. I was confused. It never occurred to me that people did it more than once a night, and Charlotte hadn't said anything about it. In the movies the sex scene always dissolved into the next day. I was amazed. So we made love again. This time he didn't fall asleep right away. He asked me how I was doing. "Fine," I said, and we cuddled and dozed off until morning.

I woke up first. Quietly, I slipped out of bed and tiptoed toward the hall closet, the only full length mirror in the apartment. I wanted to see if there was something different about me, if people would be able to tell. I looked the same.

Paul woke up and we showered and started preparing breakfast. While we were in the kitchen Rick and Charlotte emerged. The doorbell rang and Kate and Jake came in. We cracked open a few more eggs and Rick and Paul took over in the kitchen. Kate and Charlotte started to whisper. Kate mouthed to me, "did you," tilting her head in Paul's direction. I grinned and nodded. My two best friends hugged me and we all started to giggle. We were pretty obvious to the guys who smiled and slapped Paul on the back as he sliced more potatoes and turned a little red in the face. We all sat down to an enormous breakfast talking, laughing, feeling young and old all at once.

CONCLUSION
Is Virginity Important?

by Dr. Barry McCarthy
American University and Washington Psychological Center

Virginity is not the crucial factor in sexual development. Struggles about virginity usually confuse rather than elucidate important sexual and relationship learnings. Indeed, Dennis Dailey is correct in his assertion that you are a sexual person from the day of birth to the day of death. You don't have to earn sexual rights or prove anything to anyone. Sexuality is a good thing and an integral part of you as a person. The healthy question is how and when to express sexuality so as to enhance your life and relationships rather than having it be a source of anxiety, guilt, and negative experiences. I think of premarital sexuality and intercourse as training and learning to live life as a fully-functioning sexual person.

The issue for the reader is how to make personally relevant choices about sexuality which will be healthy now and in the future. Virginity and first intercourse are such intense and powerful emotional experiences that it is hard to address them in a logical, decisive manner. The first person stories in this book pointedly illustrate the complexity and individual differences which go into losing virginity and how that affects self-esteem, life, sexuality, and relationships.

What Adolescents and Young Adults Need to Learn About Sexuality

Perhaps the most important item to learn is that life gets better after 25. When I teach the "Human Sexual Behavior" course at American University, I assure my students there is "sex after A.U." Our culture places too much emphasis on sex and youth, promotes the myth that sex equals intercourse, that sex and love are the same, and that sex proves or builds love. The fantasy model of sex from movies, TV and songs exemplifies sex as spontaneous, passionate, easy, and perfect. In reality, first intercourse experiences are filled with high expectations, performance anxiety, awkwardness, little communication or planning, lack or haphazard use of birth control, and disappointment. Although no one admits it, approximately one in four males has a failed first intercourse—usually because of ejaculation before the penis is in the vagina, difficulty with erection or never attaining orgasm. Less than five percent of women are orgasmic on their first intercourse. More typically the female is confused and disappointed by how fumbling and quick it is and the amount of blood and pain. She doesn't know whether to blame herself or her partner. It's a waste of time to focus on blame; it's normal for first experiences to be uncomfortable.

What can be learned from adolescent and young adult sexual experiences which facilitates healthy adult sexuality? One crucial concept is that the more knowledgeable, comfortable, and aware you are, the better your sexual decisions. Knowledge is power; ignorance does not promote healthy sexuality. A second concept is that psychologically, intellectually, and sexually, there are many more similarities than differences between men and women. To form an intimate, stable adult relationship both people have to unlearn the dating/sex game roles. Healthy sexuality involves both people being able to comfortably discuss feelings, value a relationship, initiate sex as well as say no, and enjoy sexual expression, arousal, and orgasm.

A third major concept is the ability to accept and deal with negative or traumatic sexual experiences and not let them control your sexuality. Whether the experience is child sexual abuse, unwanted pregnancy, sexually transmitted disease, sexual assault, sexual humiliation or rejection, being the victim of exhibitionism, voyeurism, or obscene phone calls, guilt over masturbation or fantasies, sexual dysfunction or feelings of inadequacy, or uninvited physical contact in a crowd, negative sexual experiences are a normal part of sexual development. By age 25, 95% of both men and women have experienced a negative, confusing or traumatic sexual incident. How the person lost his/her virginity is sometimes that experience. Punishing oneself, feeling guilt or shame, and/or going to the extremes of denying sexuality or being indiscriminate by acting out sexuality is not healthy. You can accept negative experiences, learn from them, and proceed with pride in having survived rather than feeling like a victim. You can regain control and responsibility for your sexuality.

Valuing sexuality as an ongoing part of adult life is healthy. Only about one in four teenagers can imagine their parents having intercourse, and only one in thirteen can imagine their grandparents being sexual. As people age, comfort with sexuality and the quality of sexual experiences improve. Like everything in life, practice, feedback, and developing your own style increases enjoyment. Sexual experiences help you learn about yourself, the other gender, and relationships so you can choose a healthy, mature, intimate relationship. Although new relationships promote exciting sex, most couples realize that emotional intimacy and security increase sexual satisfaction. Sexuality can be enjoyed in your twenties, thirties, forties, fifties, sixties and beyond—an optimistic and exciting prospect.

Forming a Sexual Friendship
Although possible, it not likely you will marry the person who shared your virginity. A generation ago the average age of first intercourse was 17 for males and 19 for females. The average age to marry was 23 for males and 21 for females. In 1993, the average age of first intercourse is 16 for males and 17 for females, but the average age for marriage is 26 for males and 24 for females. Marriage researchers believe this trend to delay marriage until the mid-twenties is positive. Even more important is waiting at least two years before having a child. Couples who marry in their teens when the female is pregnant have a divorce rate of over 75% Couples who marry in their mid-twenties, spend two years developing a strong, intimate bond, and then have a planned, wanted child have divorce rates of less than 35%.

The choice of partner for first intercourse can be based on being "sexual friends." The essence of friendship is people helping and trusting each other so as to avoid hurt. Hopefully, it would be a life-time friend, but many friendships do end. Ideally, you will have a warm spot in your heart for this friend. It would be nice to have good memories of your first intercourse experience and partner.

An expert in adolescent sexuality, Dr. Sol Gordon, has a famous adage: "If you're not ready to communicate about contraception and preventing sexually transmitted diseases, you're not ready to have intercourse." He is a strong spokesman for adolescent sexuality including being comfortable with masturbation, enjoying touching and stimulation, being knowledgeable and responsible, and having an awareness of the positive functions of sexuality. Although an advocate for adolescent sexual expression, he counsels against adolescent intercourse. Risk of unwanted pregnancy and sexually transmitted diseases are higher the earlier a person begins intercourse. Approximately one in three women have an unwanted premarital pregnancy, and the rate of sexually transmitted diseases (STDs) is highest in the age range 15-19. With the advent of HIV/AIDS, the new and very real fear is that sex can cause death. This is not what friends do to each other. Sexuality is about choice, mutuality, responsibility, and sharing pleasure.

Female vs. Male Sexual Socialization

One of the most important sexual learnings is the equity between male and female. The core of a successful adult relationship is respect, trust, and emotional and sexual intimacy. In adolescence there are wide disparities between women and men. For males, sexual expression is promoted as a symbol of masculinity. No male over 15 will admit to being a virgin, although more than half are. The macho image portrays a real man willing to have sex with any woman, any time and in any situation. During adolescence the double standard, whereby the male is entitled to unlimited partners before marriage, but the female must remain a virgin, clearly favors males, but in the long run harms male psychological and sexual development. The double standard is harmful to women because they are the ones who become pregnant, are victims of sexual violence, coercion, and pressure. STDs are "sexist." Women are less likely to show symptoms so are dependent on their partner to inform them of the need to be tested and treated. The negative consequences of STDs, especially for reproduction, are severe. Young women who have intercourse with multiple partners are at higher risk for developing cervical cancer. HIV/AIDS is a sexist disease in that it is approximately 17 times easier to pass the virus from male to female than from female to male. Sperm is a powerful medium of transmission and vaginal and anal intercourse are more risky for women than men. This underscores the necessity of using condoms at each and every intercourse and the importance of disclosing HIV risk and undergoing voluntary testing. This is not meant to promote fear or paranoia, but to increase awareness of the health risks of sexuality and reinforce the need for males and females to be respectful, trusting sexual friends.

The Decision-Making Process

The most important guideline for mental health is: "Do not fool yourself." Unfortunately, when it comes to virginity and sexuality, there is little wisdom from parents, peers, and the media. This book, with its complex, personal, and moving stories presents a range of realities to enable understanding and acceptance of sexuality. Once again, in the whole spectrum of one's sexual development, virginity is not the crucial element.

Attitudes, experience, and emotions about first intercourse are important. A healthy guideline is to view sexuality as a positive part of yourself and express it in a way that enhances your life and relationship. At a minimum, this means trying to avoid behavior that is harmful to you or your partner—unwanted pregnancy, STDs, HIV/AIDS, sexual victimization and force or coercion. Hopefully, it means being a sexual friend who is aware and responsible, and who chooses to share his or her virginity in a way which will provide a positive experience and memory. If this turns out not to be the case, you can, nevertheless, learn from first intercourse so it does not negate your sexuality. Do not forget that adolescent and young adult sexuality is a training/learning process. The goal is to become an aware, comfortable, sexually functional, and intimate adult.

AVOCUS PUBLISHING—OTHER BOOKS
Edited By Louis M. Crosier

Casualties of Privilege: Essays on Prep Schools Hidden Culture $14.95
Softcover ISBN:0-9627671-0-7 (Now in its fourth printing)

Casualties of Privilege is a powerful, indeed unprecedented look inside the world of elite boarding schools. Insiders, outsiders, black and white, these former students tell their stories of life within the peer culture of some of America's best prep schools. These are stories about drinking, drugs and sex. They are also stories about friendship, trust and loyalty. Most of all, they are stories about striving to fit in, about yearning to grow up, and about managing, or mismanaging the extraordinary academic expectations of families, teachers and society at large.

Healthy Choices, Healthy Schools: The Residential Curriculum $19.95
Softcover ISBN:0-9627671-1-5

Healthy Choices, Healthy Schools combines the valuable insights of experienced boarding school heads, deans faculty members and admission directors as they examine pressing issues facing boarding schools in the 1990s. The book advances the dialogue begun by *Casualties of Privilege*. It presents concrete recommendations for improving residential life at prep school including examples of proven systems and strategies for enhancing dormmaster effectiveness. *Healthy Choices, Healthy Schools* celebrates the variety of existing residential structures and seeks to share "great ideas" so schools can learn from each other to better address contemporary educational issues.

G rowing up as a Hmong boy in the mountains of Laos, I would listen to folk tales told by the people of my village. When my cousins and I were tired of playing games, we would sit together on the ground and take turns retelling the folk tales we heard the night before.

Because the school I attended was far away from home, I would also hear new and amazing folk tales from my classmates. I made sure I remembered each one, so I could repeat them to my friends when I returned home.

When my grandparents came to visit, my siblings and I would beg them to tell us folk tales. With a bed full of attentive listeners, my grandparents took turns telling folk tales until we all fell asleep.

The folk tales I remember the best are the ones told by my mother. While preparing dinner, in order to calm down us hungry children, my mother would tell us scary folk tales. My siblings and I would listen with great interest and excitement.

These folk tales are precious Hmong treasures passed down from countless generations. It is my desire to preserve these folk tales that I grew up with in this book. They are an important part of our proud culture that I hope will never disappear.

Yakao Yang